THE
RADIANT
WOMAN
Shines

REIGNITING YOUR SPARK THROUGH
LIFE'S EBBS AND FLOWS

MARLA SACKS

The Radiant Woman Shines
Reigniting Your Spark Through Life's Ebbs and Flows

ISBN: 979-8-9906867-8-6 (Paperback)
ISBN: 979-8-9928630-3-1 (Hardcover)

Book Design by Transcendent Publishing
www.transcendentpublishing.com

Author Photography by Village Studio
www.villagestudiophotos.com

Disclaimer: The information provided in this book is not intended to
substitute for professional medical advice, diagnosis, or treatment. Please
consult your medical professional before making any changes to your
diet, exercise routine, medical regimen, lifestyle, or mental health care.

While the author has endeavored to accurately recreate events, locales,
and conversations from her memories, some details such as physical
properties and places of residence may have been changed.

Printed in the United States of America.

When one candle's flame lights another, it gets stronger. This simple but profound yogic teaching reminds us to keep shining, no matter our circumstances. The shared light never dims our own. When we share love from our hearts, our collective radiance keeps growing. Each woman's joy that sparks another life lives on forever.

TABLE OF CONTENTS

For Vanessa. Your effervescent fairy dust brightens our world, as does the image of you wearing a red raincoat on gloomy days. Though you're no longer here, you still embody love, kindness, and gentle cheer with powerful presence. You remain the epitome of The Radiant Woman, cascading her SUPER-CONSCIOUS eternal light.

PREFACE

On a dark, dismal day in February of 2004, I approached the office of a therapist recommended to me by our family pediatrician. I was meeting with her to see if she'd be a good fit for my younger son, who, along with his siblings, had been driving me a bit mad. Once "buzzed in," I turned the metal knob on a white wooden door, walked in, and quickly sat on one of the six rust-colored chairs in a U formation in one corner of the room.

After exchanging an awkward smile with another waiting mom and child, my eyes gazed downward in embarrassment for being there. I wondered what had brought this child to the office space, shared by various independent practitioners, and whether the therapy path would help shift my own distress within my family dynamic.

For what seemed like forever, I sat fidgeting in my seat and pulling at dry skin around my fingernails, my mind teeming with questions. *I loved being a mom, so why did I feel sad and frustrated? Could this therapist work with my son and guide me to manage my angst?* Finally, I heard a door open and watched another woman walk by. My heart immediately started to pound. I made sure not to make eye contact with the passerby, fearing she might know me, my story, and my secret of being unable to manage my emotions around the kids. Or worse, that my actual emotional state would be found out. Looking back, I wonder who I was truly hiding from, and I can't help but think it was myself.

Melanie, the therapist, must have picked up on my tension as I voiced concerns about my kids – two boys sandwiched between two girls, with an eight-year spread from oldest to youngest. To my surprise, I released some unexpected tears by the end of that initial fifty-minute session. Melanie said that from what she gathered, all my children seemed well-adjusted regarding their peers and peers' parents, teachers, coaches, and instructors of extracurricular activities. She assured me we could revisit my concerns about my son's persistent, resistant, and curious behavior at another time.

Humm, I thought to myself when she asked if I wanted to schedule another session. *Is one-to-one therapy meant for me? What is my missing link?*

Melanie permitted me to reveal my feeling of overwhelm. Although the appointment had gone differently than I intended, I told her I would return.

Regaining my powerful presence beyond motherhood had been the furthest thing from my mind, and yet, with each visit, I felt better. All the while, as we met weekly, later biweekly, and, eventually, monthly, I kept her a secret from everyone I knew, save my husband. I felt embarrassed and ashamed for talking with a therapist.

About a year after having our first daughters, my friend Ilene and I had driven into the woods of Neversink, New York to relax. The groovy, rustic, no-frills New Age health spa offered fresh air and massages – the perfect momma getaway. While Ilene slept in each morning, I rose with the sun, went for nature walks, and encountered my first yoga classes before breakfast. I also took outdoor Tai Chi – a non-competitive martial arts form known to reduce tension, improve cardio-vascular health and balance, and manage pain. Walking barefoot on the earth and attending restorative yoga classes in the evening helped me feel calmer. Through self-examination, great fortune arose.

Years would pass before I found another incredible entry point to yoga aside from gyms and vacations. MeriLynn's mind-body-spirit *Peaceful Yoga* classes, held in a church, served my soul. MeriLynn had a humble presence. Her joyful energy, honest life experiences, humor, and storytelling put me at ease. Yet it would be even further down the line before I was regularly trusting my intuition, prioritizing my mental and physical health when life got busy, venturing out in nature, pausing my fast-paced life to express gratitude for the moment, and integrating yoga bliss into my daily life.

During a session, Melanie, who's also a yogi, recommended two local yoga studios for me. Upon entering one, *Naturally Yoga*, I felt nervous and out of place amongst forty unfamiliar chattering students. That lonesome feeling dissipated once I heard my name called from a diagonal spot across the long gallery classroom. Not only did Dr. Gail deliver three of my four babies, but we also had a unique friendship since meeting through my college roommate's husband. In an instant, I was comforted by her warm presence. After we hugged and spoke briefly, I got props (blanket, blocks, and straps) and returned to my yoga mat. Side-by-side colorful mats lined the walls with two rows facing inward and toward one another.

Once the studio owner, who had checked me in, left her front office seat, all chatter ceased. Sheryl sat at the front of the class on a blanket and meditation cushion with her legs crossed. Everyone's attention faced her. From the moment she spoke, I felt soothed. Her gentle voice and *dharma* (which I later learned were the initial words of wisdom shared at the beginning of a traditional bhakti (devotional) yoga class) reassured me of being there. Yoga has been westernized by some who practice it only for physical movement. Sheryl's wise woman yoga teachings extended beyond a stream of flowing poses. Many stemmed from mystical aspects of Eastern Hindu culture. Her themed classes championed compassion for all beings, even "those people" in our lives who tested our limits.

It seemed like she knew what I was thinking each time I walked through the doors.

Sheryl's notable classes featured heartfelt playlists with Western and Eastern influences, incorporating lyrics, mantras, and live music. *Kirtan events*, a call-and-response devotional singing/chanting, uplifted my mood, opened my heart, and brought me inner peace. I later learned that the Beatles' White Album music was influenced by their extended ashram stays in India's spiritual culture and Kirtan music.

Rhythmic melodies resonated deeply with me as did chords played on the harmonium, a Hindu wooden instrument with keys often used in ceremonies. (Think half-sized organ on a floor with its bellowing sounds). From brass clanging chimes to a gong's reverberation, the orchestrated instruments enveloped me in their immersive atmosphere. Similar to how I felt when organs, pianos, and bells sounded or vocals were sung in a place of worship, be it a holy temple or church. Franz Schubert's "Ave Maria" has always made my heart sing at a Catholic wedding or funeral, as does "*Adon Alam*," often sung at the end of a Saturday service in the temple. The spirited music's lasting effect lingered long after the service. After class ended, I often found myself humming vibrational tunes all the way home.

A few years later, I'd learned enough harmonium chords, using the keyboard and bellows to produce sound when I taught yoga.

Classes often began with an invocation mantra (sound currents to bathe our minds). Sheryl would then invite us to fold over into a child's pose (toes together, knees bent out, buttocks toward the heels, breathing into the back body, lowering our head to the Earth). The fragrance of incense and burning candles pierced my heart and awakened my soul into a new multidimensional sensory system.

Next, layers of overwhelm began to dissipate. The experience went from a physical practice to a complete emotional release within a short time.

Therapy helped me understand myself in the context of my family's woven relations. Practicing yoga widened my appreciation for all beings. I recognized their potential for grander lives by acknowledging the power of connecting mind, body, and spirit. As I embraced conscious learning, spiritual signs – always present but not obvious – revealed themselves to me.

An enlivened sensation, bliss, began to permeate my bloodstream. Beauty went beyond the surface. My spiritual connections became more profound as I delved deeper. Raw, intricate patterns were uncovered, revealing precious treasures. I felt wholesome, purified, and holier than I ever felt before. I broke through separation barriers founded on falsified differences I once believed. The progression fed new meaning and purpose into my life.

The search for peace opened my eyes to spiritual
awesomeness. Each yoga posture and meditation
class filled my heart with a ferocious appetite
for abundant love.

I felt courageous when turning upside down in downward dog; rooting and rising in warrior one, two and three; and lifting my heart higher than my head as I bowed forward in child's pose. Though some postures were known as "apex" (when we build up to an inversion-like headstand or *Vrksasana* – crow pose), most flows are created at the teacher's discretion. Students can research class descriptions before signing up. High-intensity and gentle options are available for all levels.

Hatha yoga (practiced at a slower pace) focuses on our breath, controlled movements, and stretching. *Vinyasa* yoga, which connects the breath to our movements, tends to be set faster. *Kundalini* – or life force awareness – yoga incorporates mantra, meditation, movement, and mudras for an unexpected full-body experience. Combining each of those ascending practices into my life filled me with extra focus, determination, contentment, and abundance.

Most traditional yoga classes (though, as mentioned, they differed depending on the student/teacher) led to *savasana* (resting or "corpse" pose). In that final phase of the class, after we stretched on the floor and twisted for seated posture, the students were invited to integrate the experience into the five to ten minutes of relaxation. Savasana strengthens and releases our muscles before we re-enter the world.

Yoga *asanas* (poses) and meditation practices taught me to recover my self-worth and let go of fear. Sitting, walking, and taking any action to engage in a meditation practice consciously is known to have many overall benefits for our well-being (lowers cortisol as it decreases stress). It permitted me to stop striving to fit into societal expectations of who I was supposed to be. My actions in private were the same as in public, allowing me to find clarity with new direction to embrace every polarity of life. One day after a class, I was home in my backyard and looked at a spider, her yellow and gold body purposely moving in the organized web she'd constructed. At that moment, I knew I was hooked on the yogic lifestyle for it allowed me to notice nature's simple yet awesome and spectacular moments. Everything in our lives, even the little critters, bestows purpose and presence.

I recall receiving weekly allergy shots when I was a teen. Little bits of ragweed, pollen, and histamine were administered to make me less reactive to them. Although some of those reactions abated for years, other environmental allergies and food sensitivities appeared as I aged. Inflammation multiplied.

While witnessing specific symptoms, I realized it was time to reevaluate my approach to healthcare. A holistic approach to healing can be enhanced by cultivating awareness of the body's energy and radiance. When we experience inflammatory markers, contentious turmoil, or hormonal imbalances, it alerts us to make changes in our thoughts, habits, and lifestyles. Gratitude for the present moment steered me to manage my sensitivities better. When on my yoga mat and afterward, I rallied for my hindered self, knowing I could contribute to its wellbeing. The more I became intuitive, the better I understood what was ailing myself and others.

Overreactive bodies are universal precursors for a highly inflamed state, from the foods we eat to the information we digest.

Why did leaders of certain religious denominations or governments use their power to induce followers instead of giving them tools to ignite individual empowerment and happy spiritedness? Some institutions or chosen faiths produce compliant patrons over spiritual growth.

When our starlight shines, we reap the benefits as seers of majestic planes, hills, landscapes, and planets that are immeasurable yet attainable to reach through intuitive measures at any moment.

I wanted to feel better and be accepted and loved in this quest. Access the power within and around me that lets me be the real me – finding fulfillment through freedom of the body and mind. Not bound to anybody or anything except for the ebbs and flows of life. Living in a materialistic world

– and being a lover of beautiful fashion, designer jeans, and homes – I knew that a Gucci bag didn't buy happiness. We can deepen our higher self by sweetening our lives with experiential nectar instead of glossing over our emotional state with merchandise. When our style is influenced by intuition, we rise to and fro with foresight. This measure translates as truth even when we hit rock bottom moments because the universal truth supports all beings.

Searching to understand the human experience, I observed social climbers who faked radiance by surrounding themselves in the luxury of middle- to upper-class circles and designer bags, wanting to look twenty and thirty again or like the women in magazines, and whose mental states and insecurities had them drinking and gossiping to excess.

I craved deeper connection and uncovered it – and my true essence – through radiance yoga and meditation, which celebrate your victories as well as mine. This discovery awakened the Radiant Woman lying dormant inside me, and I bet there is a Radiant Woman waiting inside of you, too. My hope is that by sharing my story, you'll look within and find her.

The Radiant Woman in me welcomes you!

Introduction

WHEN A RADIANT WOMAN LOSES HER GRIP AND FINDS HER HEART

On a blind date with a mystery man standing six feet tall and wearing black cowboy boots and a big grin, I remember thinking, *This may be who I've been searching for my entire life.* He introduced himself as Jonathan ("Jon," growing up) and told me he was from Pennsylvania, Ohio, and Rhode Island. As he shared stories from his roots, his eyes lit up when speaking about his younger, and already married, brother. I grew curious about his family and wondered if I would meet them in the future. After a few days of waiting in anticipation, he called me again. From there, we dined out on Italian and Chinese; we found a favorite in the German apple pancake at The Ritz Diner. Some mornings, he would pick me up from my parents' home for a 5:30 a.m. weight training workout at Diamond Gym, a lowkey body-building joint in Irvington, New Jersey. Together, we fell in love with *The Phantom of the Opera* and saw it many times over. The more I fell in love, the more I fell in love with listening to his music, from Elvis' "Love Me Tender" to Guns and Roses' "Patience" and dancing on his shoulders all night at Kiss concerts. We saw The Stones together in California. He got on board with me being a Jersey girl – and loyal lover of Bruce Springsteen. As our relationship budded, I made homemade tomato sauce and lasagna for him, and he made fluffy pancakes from a box for me.

Our first trip together was a Caribbean cruise over New Year's Eve. We went to the South of France and Paris on our next excursion, which coincided with my birthday. I thought he might pop the question then, and when it did happen, he caught me totally off guard. It was an ordinary Monday night. After a workout, Jonathan drove me home in his black Chevy Tahoe. While we sat in my driveway gazing out the window, he proposed. At first, I didn't believe what I heard – we were wearing T-shirts and sweats, not looking at each other! – then I saw the ring he was holding near my finger. I said yes without hesitation.

Our sweeping love led to one blistering hot day that became a magical night. I recall trembling with delight as I walked down the aisle at sundown, a dove white and blush-colored rose bridal bouquet in my hands. The creamy white wedding gown with its long-sleeved lace bodice, train and bustle made me feel like a princess. After exchanging rings and personalized vows – *"You will be my best friend and I yours..."* – our attendees wished us *Mazel Tov* (congratulations on a *Simcha* – lifecycle) in unison – the groom stomped one foot on a glass as customary in Jewish weddings. This joyous ritual marked the official beginning of our marriage, where we committed to a life of happiness while withstanding hardships together. It set the tone for a moment of reflection on the meaning of marriage, both in times of prosperity and adversity. This is like the destruction and reconstruction of Jewish temples in ancient times. We then locked eyes and kissed with excitement anticipating our future together (and, of course, the reception – a roaring party of two hundred and fifty that went well past midnight, with a brunch to follow the next day).

Jonathan mapped out our entire honeymoon, which, as I was sensitive to the sun, was not the common beach destination but an exploration. We had both developed a love for travel, mine beginning the year I studied abroad in college.

The first part of our trip was on land. We visited The Crown Jewels at The Tower of London, shopped at the iconic seven-storied department store, Harrods, for crystal, fine porcelain china, and clothing, and went to the theater twice – all of it picture-perfect despite the on-and-off rain the UK is known for. The night we saw *Five Guys Named Moe* is ingrained in my mind. We were enjoying the show (and trying to ignore the heat in the theater, which was cooled only with forced air) when suddenly I was a part of it when I was called on stage! It was an incredible moment I will never forget.

We then rented a car and headed out of the hustle and bustle of the city to a region known for its idyllic beauty – the Cotswolds. After a few days in the most charming inn, we went to Devon's horse country, with its cobblestoned beaches and green pastures of grazing sheep. We even played croquet.

The second part of our honeymoon was a cruise destined for Denmark, Amsterdam, Stockholm, and Russia (the latter a tweak from the original stop, the fjords of Norway, due to The Gulf War). As we docked in St. Petersburg (still called Leningrad then), we saw a city that appeared to be stuck in a time warp. Taxis on their last legs drove wildly down streets so dilapidated they looked like they had been recently bombed. During our visit to the Hermitage Museum, we noticed that many of the collections lacked proper ventilation and protection from the sun's rays, which could damage the rare artwork. Our next excursion, "Moscow in a Day," began with an early-morning, low-budget flight aboard a rickety plane. We were surprised to arrive amidst great fanfare. Tourists in those times were given the royal treatment. Flashing lights from motorcars and motorcycles heralded our entrance into the city of colorful domes. Police held up traffic in the intersections for our two tour buses to pass through and enter The Kremlin.

We toured many landmarks, including the domed Red Square you see on every Russian postcard. We ventured into parks where we chatted with people eager to chat with us, their eyes staring back with interest in us yet revealing something missing in their lives. We used bathrooms with rough, thin paper squares of toilet paper and pieces of bar soap too tiny for a good lather. That evening, we sat in a vast room and dined on traditional *chicken Kiev* accompanied by Russian dance performers – the entertainment, talent, and extravagant costumes a sharp contrast from the lackluster facilities we had seen throughout the day.

Each port we visited offered a crash course into the various cultures and places, leaving impressions we would carry with us forever. After nearly three incredible weeks in Europe, we returned home ready to start our new life together.

Twenty-one months after beginning our journey as husband and wife, Jonathan and I entered a new region: parenthood. Both of us adored the process – from diapering to breastfeeding and pumping so Dad could take the night shift to juggling new routines and meals out with our little pumpkin in tow. Amanda went everywhere with us – her diaper bag, equipped with toys and snacks, ready to go anytime. Onlookers were impressed with her demeanor. Though life got hectic, it came naturally to both of us.

I balanced time with family and friends with my position as a marketing and sales assistant for a stairway and elevator lift company. On some days I commuted. On others, I worked from home, outfitted with an office computer.

Next came baby number two. Jeremy's delivery took us by surprise. Soon after calling Doctor Gail, I took a long shower and shaved. I thought our little one was going to arrive much later, even after the onset of contractions, because I had labored with his big sister for well over twenty hours. Boy, was I wrong! My parents, sister, and doctor all arrived at the hospital before us, and as soon as I was whisked into my delivery room it was time to push.

Jeremy's arrival went easier than expected but he was born tongue-tied, for which he needed surgery a few months later. He bounced back and recovered, then at age two he was diagnosed with developmental speech delays. By three, he required an intensive program three times a week for apraxia – a neurological condition that affects movement – in his case, speech. For years, I brought him to various specialized speech therapists, who also instructed us on exercises to continue at home. Initially, I prayed for him to speak using multiple-syllable words, but then I hoped he would catch up with his peers verbally.

I juggled work tasks between pre-k, elementary school, and after-school carpools. Composed business emails keeping end users in mind, informed architects and physical/occupational therapists about the latest stairway/wheelchair lift models. Spreading awareness of the updated Americans with Disabilities Act, aiming to overcome public entrance barriers and make homes accessible to persons with injuries or disabilities felt essential to me. It was an honor to participate in outreach events alongside rehabilitation hospitals. Our entire product line was geared towards promoting human dignity and connection.

Dual roles became a challenge as life got busier, even with my job's flexible work hours. With little inner turmoil, I decided to give up one position and fully embrace life as a suburban mother.

On most weekdays, Jonathan left our long, winding driveway and headed to the train station fifteen minutes away, arriving an hour later at 4 World Trade Center in Lower Manhattan. A finance guy with the perfect side of fatherhood, he prospered in business and in life.

Next came baby number three. Birthing through intense back labor pain was worth it after little Benjamin was born. His beautiful, petite features and piercing brown eyes took my breath away, though seeing him hooked up to all those wires was scary. An arrhythmic heartbeat was detected when he was in my womb, necessitating a visit from a pediatric cardiologist after delivery. And, though brief, his intense, gut-wrenching colic tears stole a piece (or shall I say "peace") of my mind.

With little Ben, there was less time for everyone, and he let us know what he wanted – whether it was another "Thomas the Tank Engine" or something else that caught his eye. Even though home life was tough to manage, Jonathan and I wanted to have four children – a larger family than either of us was raised in. Less than two years later, with the arrival of Rachel, that vision became a reality. During a home expansion that included a new kitchen and two bedrooms above it so each child would eventually have a room, a guest room was kept available for visitors.

My two hands were never enough with our little sunshine, Rachel, but her adorableness made every moment worth it. Each smile and tear filled our house with audacious excitement. From family commotion to having the painter walk in on me while breastfeeding, there was nowhere to go for privacy. It seemed like Benjamin started to scream for our attention after Rachel's birth. Our family unit, though chaotic, felt complete.

Most evenings, Jonathan arrived home in time to sit down with our family for a three-course dinner that I lovingly cooked. I roasted squash for butternut soup, used Williams and Sonoma's bread-maker for fresh loaves, and adorned salads with chopped celery, grated carrots, croutons, toasted nuts, and cranberries. I also varied meat and fish recipes with pasta, rice, or potatoes—chicken cutlets or nuggets were a staple for years, as applesauce and homemade baby food to satisfy everyone's palette where applicable.

As a full-time doer, I participated in Parent-Teacher Advisor (PTA) meetings, chaperoned trips, and orchestrated snacks and craft projects for the children, including beaded jewelry for them to make their moms for Mother's Day within their classrooms and the girls' Brownies/Girl Scouts troops and the boys' Boy Scouts meetings. For the infamous Pinewood Derby nights, Jon helped them carve functioning cars that never took first place for speed but zoomed well around the tracks for events of memorable cheer and good family fun. Co-coaching Amanda's girls' lacrosse was an intense yet fulfilling commitment, as was attending each child's sports games and dance/music recitals.

To burn off steam from motherhood, I made time for fitness like kickboxing classes and sporadically popped into yoga at the gym for a touch of stretch and calm.

Then came the ordinary morning where birds chirped, the sun shone through the red jasper leaves, and a hummingbird landed on the red and clear Lucite feeder suctioned to our kitchen window.

I had just served the little ones and made breakfast-to-go for hubby.

Like most days, he kissed my cheek and said, "I love you," as I handed him a lime-green ribboned basket filled with homemade oatmeal sweetened with brown sugar and two toasted buttered egg muffins sprinkled with cinnamon and sugar on top. Everything had been prepared with love and appeared to be going as well as intended.

After having a quick fruit yogurt, I left to finish dropping off my kids at preschool. I opened the garage door with Rachel on my hip and adjusted Benjamin in his booster seat. I paused to look at my pear-shaped, almost flawless diamond engagement ring. Next, I fastened and secured his sister's car seat strap latches, and then off we went, turning right onto Forest Ave.

If anyone had peered in on me, they would have thought I had everything: the husband, the kids, a grand house, and two little white fluffy Maltese. Indeed, I was surrounded by lots of exterior beauty, complete with a robust cherry blossom tree and a pristine, landscaped lawn that matched our impeccable and faux-finished interior walls. I kept busy and was riding high.

And yet, on that seemingly ordinary Tuesday, as I drove down the winding hills of my neighborhood, I started to cry. Then, as I neared the yellow blinking light close to my neighborhood, I cried more.

This is strange, I thought. *Why do I feel blue? What is happening inside of me?*

No sooner had I passed over the railroad tracks when yet another flood of tears gushed from my eyes. I can still remember like it was yesterday the moment when, blinded, I pulled over to the side of the road. In the back seat behind me, "The Wiggles" tunes played for two little ones, neither of whom knew what was happening with their mom.

This could get quite embarrassing, I thought, the tepid tears still streaming down my cheeks, *What if a neighbor or friend notices my sandy-colored minivan as they drive by? I must gain control and gather myself!*

And so, I did.

Gripping the steering wheel tight, I braced myself, took in a few unconscious breaths, noticed where tears had drenched my sleeves, and pulled away into the traffic flow.

To anyone watching, I appeared to be going about my typical day – dropping little Ben and Rachel off at their classes, running errands, getting groceries for dinner and, later, picking the kids up and gearing up for after-school activities. It was the same when, once home, I went about our evening routine. Yet I nervously waited for things to quiet and Hubby and I were alone…

"Why were you upset when you have everything?" Jonathan asked.

I had just told him about that morning – how my emotions had erupted before I dropped the kids off. How I had been crying so hard I had to pull over. How I had suddenly felt lost and didn't know why.

His question, and what he said next, glossed over my experience and, to my dismay, confirmed that my emotions lacked merit.

"We have built a great family together. You can be home with the kids. We have enough money for food, a beautiful home, and everything else we want. A wonderful life."

I knew he was right – we did have "everything" – so where had my profound sadness, and the resulting crying jag, come from? A part of me still felt shipwrecked from the sudden panic as I bared my emotions. It seemed that after years of labor, delivery, and rote routines, my body and mind reached some tipping point.

Then I heard a small voice ask if I could travel back to my junior year of college, when I studied abroad and felt free to make my own decisions, would I do it?

It had been an incredible period of my life – when I acquired a liking for sitting alone in cafes, engaged in meaningful conversations with travelers and locals. I became a sponge for figuring things out without hesitating, even when foreign signs or languages revealed their differences. I felt safe, secure, ambitious, alive, accomplished, and accepted, no matter if I was in a cultured business, conversing with marketing professors or other students, viewing ancient sites, riding in motorcars or strolling English gardens. I absorbed extraneous information like a sponge. The everlasting experience impressed survival mode in me. Each opportunity or obstacle challenged me to grow, illuminated my spirit. I developed a taste for high tea, biscuits, and shepherd's pie; I visited pubs in Dublin, where local draft cider and Guinness brewed beer flowed on tap. I lived out an extraordinary dream in foreign lands and thrived on independence.

When my father said he would not pay one additional penny over my state university tuition a few months prior, I got resourceful and applied to the subsidized British University school system north of London, nearer to Liverpool. My determination to journey alone into the unknown unleashed my joyful spirit. It set me free to roam. And it has stood as a pinnacle point ever since.

For so long I had told myself, *That was then. This is your reality now.* I had accepted the sting of being overwhelmed ... until that day when I lost my grip. Now, I was bound and determined to get it back. My first approach, the "cover up," buried my emotional truth. Life continued. I figured, *This too shall pass.*

This lasted for a year after my unexplained cry. It felt as if a knob in me had shut off and I was on autopilot, unfeeling. I must have made an unconscious choice to harden myself. There could be no other explanation for why I no longer shed tears of sorrow – or joy, for that matter. That's when, like an answer to a prayer I didn't even know I had uttered, I met Melanie.

The motherhood juggling act was real. Yes, I had a house-keeper to keep things tidy. And yes, I had my husband, who did his share of carpooling and was hands-on with the kids after a full day's work and on weekends. But, each weekday morning, he could trade our suburban New Jersey home's rolling hills and green trees for the hustle and bustle of Lower Manhattan – and live a completely different life.

For me it had been different. When my head hit the pillow at the end of the day, I felt depleted and unaccomplished, only to wake up fearing I would never check off everything on my to-do list. And, as my family thrived, I went numb.

When Melanie closed the door behind us, I felt safe.

Her cheerful presence, warm smile, pure complexion, and black jumper and espadrille wedge sandals put me at ease. She looked relaxed yet professional, with a sparkle in her eyes. On the other hand, I felt washed out, overwhelmed by bouts of stress. Behind the scenes, I was a mess!

Melanie's nod told me she understood my anguish. It felt good to be validated.

As mentioned, I barely spoke of my relationship with her to anyone, though she was my rock during those challenging years. I was also grateful that my *worst fear* – being seen or noticed by one of Melanie's incoming or outgoing clients or some-one driving by my car, parked on the cut-through backroad of a neighboring town – never happened. Fortunately, the street was nestled amongst trees, houses, and stores.

Periodically, Hubby asked if I was "fixed" yet. Though he questioned therapy's purpose, I knew my mental health mattered. Talk therapy opened me up to expressing my emotions, while yoga offered me a new perspective. When I moved my body on my mat, I walked with peace and strength back to my car. My emotions stirred with enlivened sensations instead of dull, stagnant energy. This time, I felt safe and supported again by a bhakti (devotional love) community. Students and teachers restored my faith.

Then, one day, as I walked into Naturally Yoga, which had started to feel like my second home, I bumped into none other than Melanie! As my yogic lifestyle increased, my scheduled sessions with her had become less frequent.

At first, we exchanged a wink, a smile, or nod as we passed in the long hall, as she'd suggested should we ever see each other outside her office. On occasion, her mat was placed next to mine. As time passed, we got to know one another as students of life. Navigating our karmic (action deeds) and dharmic paths, grappling with inner struggles, reshaping our lives in the name of love.

In my quest, I was captivated by nature's abundance. I was enamored, watching bumblebees cross-pollinate the flowers, knowing when and where to go each year so my raspberry bushes multiply and bear fruit. I prioritized befriending myself as I cared for family and friends. I chanted the *Sat Nam* mantra, a sound current known to protect the mind. It means, "Your identity is truth." Each beat permeated my entire being as I strummed my soul. *Ujjayi's* "Ocean breath" flowed from one yoga pose to another, guiding me to release stagnant energy. Breath of fire, a *kundalini* awareness breath achieved by pumping the navel center in a fast-paced breathing rhythm, through the nose or a panting mouth, became the almighty driving force of my sensation and awakening.

When invoking *jappa* (Sanskrit for "repetitive mantra") with a one-hundred-eight-beaded mala necklace (similar to a rosary), I was soothed by the melodic rhythm of touching each bead while chanting silently or aloud. My mind quieted as I closed my eyes and slid one finger to the next bead while sitting on a cushion or a chair with my spine elongated. Counting those one hundred and eight beads around the looped strand rebirthed my energy.

Each peaceful state transformed my days into a spiritual roller coaster ride. So, I decided to train and got certified as a 200- and eventually 500-hour yoga alliance teacher, as well as many modalities that helped me uncover myself. Traveled to Mount Shasta, California for *Sat Nam Rasayan®* ancient arts healing; *Kripalu Yoga Center in* Lenox, Massachusetts for kundalini yoga teacher certification; *Mindfulness-Based Stressed Reduction* (MBSR) as per Jon Kabat-Zin; yoga therapeutics for cancer through Kula for Karma, and Psych-K by Rob Williams. My vitality and zeal for life increased. I reveled in human connection as the student-teacher relationship became a give-and-take experience. Breath awareness gave me wings to fly as my lungs expanded. Entrenched in meditative moments, I frequently experienced a euphoric sensation as if I were floating. Kicking up to the handstands from my youth made me fearless and invincible. After sitting in meditation, I felt like a shining warrior. Each action-oriented or calming practice readied me for victory by letting go of fear. My succession as a Radiant Woman soared.

I embraced the concept of *Namaste* (honoring the light within you as the light within me) and found expanded freedom in my relationships.

As I manifested love and light, I saw it in every being and site.

Your brilliance, like mine, can shine anywhere, anytime. For example, we can bring extraordinary peace into our day by recalling a recent walk in a park, on a beach, or in the mountains. We imbue the most straightforward facets of life with love, turning ordinary steps into walking meditation. Embrace the fantasy dream in times of struggle by allowing our true unique self to feel and transform over time.

We consciously show up with purpose through our strengths rather than our weaknesses.

Everyone is born with a zest for life, but many need help finding the shuffle. If you're in a funk or feel like crawling into a hole today, it is probably rooted in your early family connections or lack thereof.

As a young mom, I went above and beyond. Got selflessness all mixed up. I never wanted a Best Mom award banner across my head, yet I did go head over heels to guard and love my children. I was drawn to mothering my little ones into youth; however, in the interim I neglected to safeguard myself. With no other passions or depth of study to learn or stimulate me outside my circle, I naively allowed my inner spark to dim. I hadn't followed through on any other ambitions. I knew there was more; I wanted to play and be less serious with myself. I had yet to realize that a creative, poetic light was waiting for me to wake up with each sunrise. Once I became a bit "selfish" by making peace of mind a priority, life shifted for me. When we access bliss, we can transfer it to the next person we meet.

It sounds simple because it is: when we remind ourselves to turn our frown upside down, we emphasize our limitlessness.

The quickest route to feeling radiant is to never fear failure; faith, trust, and hope are just around the corner from fear and worry.

Throughout this transformation, I continued to join moms in parking lots after drop-offs and run errands and carpools, always smiling. The catalyst occurred when I envisioned change was possible.

This is why I've included The Radiant Woman's Way meditations and prompts throughout this book. Consider taking notes as you read. Air-write contemplative thoughts from your mind to move the spearhead point forward, type on a keyboard or phone, or bring your hand to paper. Releasing thoughts can be therapeutic. During the first year of my yoga teacher training (TT), I got reacquainted with journaling. Took furious notes whenever teachers shared potent life lessons such as relinquishing attachment to any scene or mood because life changes in a snap. Whatever we can do to get thoughts out of our head – be it on paper or canvas, while playing an instrument or sport, listening to music, or partaking in any art form – gives us the moment to express emotions, experience presence, release, and shine.

Tempt the creative woman within to channel her muse, capture life's joy, to feel better. Integrate calming and energetic processes as levers to get unstuck.

You've got this, my friend. Keep reading and rising!

Chapter 1

BEAUTY COMES FROM WEAR AND TEAR (AND TEARS)

"You have been criticizing yourself for years, and it hasn't worked. Try approving of yourself and see what happens."

~ Louise L. Hay

Fashion significantly influenced me while growing up in the New Jersey suburbs outside Philadelphia. Like many young girls, I wanted to look like the women who appeared on the covers and pages of fashion magazines, and I have vivid memories of their groovy bell bottoms, clip-on dangling earrings, and neon, floral-patterned shirts popular in the '70s. Perhaps those cover-girl images and familiar faces deceived me. They appeared happy and content, as did the real-life women in my life. Indeed, I also aspired to be like my well-dressed mom, her friends, and my older cousins and aunts. Dad wore big buckle belts and wide, horizontal-striped tops when he wasn't suited for work. Together, my parents were a hipster-looking couple sporting the polyester threads of their times.

I went from playing dress-up to going shopping with Mom. She impressed upon me the importance of matching clothing articles – from purses and shoes to underwear and tights. She taught me to accessorize, choosing the perfect jewelry and other items to finish my outfits. Aunt Arlene (her sister, younger by nine-plus years) taught me how to put on makeup.

While preparing for my first year of high school, my family and I relocated to northern New Jersey. As a teen, denim, sweatshirts, corduroy, and flannel put me at ease, but I loved to sparkle for occasions like sweet sixteens and New Year's Eve. One of my favorite weekend activities was shopping for vintage and trendy clothing at local malls or venturing to Canal Street in New York City. Sometimes I felt pressure to conform to societal beauty standards and seek approval from my friends, but I also discovered my personal style.

From youth into womanhood, trousseau to cruise wear, my taste for finer things expanded. I bought my bridal shoes and my first pair of Manolos (beyond comfortable!) at Bergdorf's. Our home was filled with upscale kitchen products and bedroom linens. I served delectable multicourse meals to friends and family on china plates, with appetizers on sterling silver platters.

I had a knack for following and mastering recipes, adding signature touches to simple and complex dishes like my mother-in-law's apple crumble pie and Mom's *kugel* (a sweet noodle pudding and Jewish staple side dish assembled with egg noodles, cottage cheese, crushed pineapple, butter, cinnamon, and sugar, with a butter and sweetness browned top for an extra crunch). I also prepared ratatouille (tomato, oregano, and summer squash); tapenade (roasted eggplant, olives, and capers), and red sauces, including one that called for briefly boiling the fruit (known as blanching) and then peeling the tomato skin so it would be less bitter.

These efforts were encouraged and validated by the compliments of family and friends, who frequently spoke of the warmth they felt when they walked through our front door.

Every detail was carefully ensured to be perfect, down to the matching napkins, placemats, and table settings. My to-do lists for decorating, shopping, cooking, and tending to others was never-ending. I sometimes stressed right before people arrived for birthday parties or other celebrations and got snappy with the ones I loved before our guests arrived. After all was said and done, I felt less accomplished than anticipated.

Despite all the luxuries and support around me, I freely gave my peace away. Being a people-pleaser thinned my energy.

With the accumulation of bedroom furniture, decorative needlepoint pillows, gold and silver gilded frames, sterling silver candlestick holders, plus a playroom filled with toys, a part of me felt empty, with no space to breathe. My exterior world appeared idyllic but my mind's internal landscape teetered on imbalance. And, though I didn't like admitting it to my husband, I knew he was right that on days leading up to and during my menstrual cycle, my overwhelm amplified.

There must be another way, I thought, *to care for myself and manage my mood shifts, fears, and expectations.*

I first paid attention to my higher self while on a health and wellness retreat a year after my older daughter turned one. I recall wanting to bottle up the new perception I gained from that experience and incorporate it into my young family. However, years later, on the brink of collapse by the side of the road, my struggle became a pinnacle point. When we face our obstacles (rather than ignore them), we give ourselves renewed reason to rise and shine!

Meditating at ambrosial hours (before the sun rose and as it set) gave me a reasonable chance to adopt a progressive yoga lifestyle. In gradual increments, my physical and mental health well-being improved. I upped my spiritual mind-body fitness routines and turned life into an ambitious game. This didn't mean I erased pain or forgot what being different, alienated, or left out felt like. Instead, I purified my body and mind by awakening the tremendous innate spirit from within to rise regularly.

Infusing Mantra Moments Into My Day

I paid attention to nature's glory. A walk in the park felt better than buying a new pair of shoes.

The "stripped down" minimalist accepts herself without attachments before considering external objects of desire.

We truly succeed when we prioritize our goals and values over emulating others. Do we care if we have a fancy new car or do we feel like we ought to fit in with everyone else on the block? Do we even want to buy those designer jeans because all our friends have a pair?

Trying to "keep up with the Joneses" is a losing battle. Someone else sets the bar even higher whenever we think we are close. A newer, cooler model emerges when we buy the latest gadget or device. Once our kitchen is remodeled, a new home trend will take over, and we will be slightly outdated. I have fallen into this trap as well. It's important to remember that it's okay to want and make changes that uplift our spirits if our decisions are based solely on what we want and can afford. Rather than keeping up with society's standards of commercialism and consumerism, we should focus on making choices that align with our values and bring us true happiness.

Many women cover up their emotions with external noise – often, that noise concerns social ideals about their appearance. They strive to be called "beautiful or elegant" rather than fulfilling their inner aptitude. Each woman wears her unique hat yet, at the same time, wants to fit in and be accepted. Searching for immediate attention and approval can turn an otherwise wise woman blind. Seeking outward validation *tarnishes* our looks in the form of glazed eyes. Addictive behaviors can form because we lack the tools to deal with our emotions. Unresolved conflicts within ourselves and in our relationships can create frown lines. There's a difference between a smile crease and a frown's wrinkle, and it shows by the sparkle in one's eyes instead of one's glossed-over appearance.

When true beauty is revived, it winks with confident direction. Abundant waterfalls unite her with a fountain of youth, her original self, born again in an image of love.

As I have attested, keeping up with the demands of our larger culture – whatever it may be – can be exhausting. And, just as I did, multitasking women with burdensome layers can reinvent their purpose through conscious connections. When pressured by life challenges, the curious woman dips her toes into new facets.

Self-realization silenced my inner critic, enabling me to befriend the once-upon-a-time little girl and her two crooked front teeth. Through a new lens, my almond-shaped brown eyes viewed – and appreciated – suburban living near New York City. The external recreations in an urban world of fashion, epicurean spas, gourmet food, Broadway shows, music, avant-garde arts and people of varied cultural backgrounds nourished me, as did the happiness after a heart-to-heart talk with a friend.

Women can strengthen their bonds by supporting one another, avoiding comparing themselves to each other, and developing a deeper trust in their intuition. We reject unrealistic standards when we make eye contact with ourselves in the mirror, rather than trying to control the uncontrollable (i.e., comparing yourself to your five-foot-ten roommate when you're five-foot-one). Yes, that is part of my story. If only my legs were long enough to scan the crowded party room or see above the taller heads at the theater! By accepting what God or a Higher Power has given us, we can navigate the operations of our bodies, like a motor vehicle that requires maintenance but is not attempting to become a different model.

Life's neither a one-way upward ticket to paradise nor a nonstop rollercoaster of adventure and thrills, but it can be beautiful if you seek it without expectations. In "blue zone" cities/towns/villages worldwide, families gather, live near each other, cook healthy meals, and walk amongst homes and nature as a means of fitness. Studies of people born and raised in these hot spots prove they not only live longer (one-hundred-plus years is commonplace) but are some of the happiest, most content people on our planet. They are not measured by

BMI (body mass index), weight, or waistline. Their concept of body image was less distorted by social trends and more influenced by health as its wealthy companion.

Many women distort their image, only to note years later when they see a picture of themselves that they didn't look bad (and perhaps even looked quite lovely). Throughout my life, I have fallen victim to the self-critic and comparison route. It's not easy to be comfortable in our body size and shape when perfection is misaligned – it can even lead to eating disorders.

Relying upon inherent factors (hair, nails, shoes, bags) to make me feel good was a price to pay before blanketing myself in self-love and prioritizing mind tools to release the body tension, anger, and frustrations festering inside me.

Once we consciously choose to navigate the trenches of our lives by befriending ourselves, we find happiness amid calamities.

Airbrushing and app filters certainly don't help matters. I recall meeting someone in person after several months of virtual meetings and not recognizing her! This is not a judgment; I have also used Zoom's lip highlighter effect and had professional photos retouched. Intense magnification from high-resolution cameras can distort our perception of one another by making wrinkles appear more pronounced or erased. Cultural preferences often undervalue and mask women's authentic beauty. Improving ourselves to feel our best in every phase begins with acceptance, less judgment/resentment, whether about pre-menstrual hormones or the sagging skin that accompanies aging. Dysmorphia and other appearance-related disorders can occur when we disconnect from ourselves in private, perhaps from trying to appropriate our appearance in public. How do we intercept compulsive urges before we overeat, purge, shop, think, and speak? How do we repair dysfunctional behaviors generated by our emotions when psychological habits are triggered?

We all rely on ingrained stimuli to boost our mood. Which option would better suit us when we're faced with an obstacle or have some leisure time? Get in the habit of asking, "What do I need right now?" when searching for an answer from within.

When we feel unhappy or troubled, our subconscious mind tends to rebel. When we dismiss or stifle ourselves from true expression, we exacerbate our feelings because the original uncomfortable memory recalls the incident and the pain we're causing ourselves by reliving the distorted past.

We may need to take a walk to feel energized, nap to feel better rested, practice deep breathing to clear our head, or drink some water to hydrate ourselves.

Remember, we are the creators of our lives, women born to be healthy, free-spirted, and wise.

The Radiant Woman's Way

It is always possible to activate your radiance.

If you struggle with self-acceptance or body image, consider incorporating fitness activities, self-help books, contemplation, meditation, and journaling into your routine.

Note the things you've done well, the choices you've made that you're proud of, the progress you've made, and even the things that require no action at all – for example, the time you gave yourself to *be*.

If you're feeling down or doubting yourself, try asking, "What does my body need? What does my mind need? What does my spirit need right now?" Or "What can I do to accentuate my radiance, health and balance now?"

Self-validation is expressing where you are in the moment and redirection depends on you.

> *Keeping a gratitude journal can help establish a habit of appreciation for the good things in life we encounter.*

Things to consider for your thankfulness "check-in": designate time each day, midday or before bed, and set a reminder.

If you don't write with pen to paper or type it in your phone notes, you can still take a few minutes daily to give yourself some credit – a literal or figurative pat on the back.

The main thing here is not to write the same thing twice:i.e. "I am grateful for my family; I am thankful for the sun. I am full of gratitude for lettuce growing in my garden. I loved the poached egg power bowl with shitake and avocado I ate at *Mindful Café*. I appreciate my husband putting the roof rack on our car and packing the boogie boards and beach chairs for our annual trip to Maine."

Now you try:

I am grateful for_____

I am thankful for_____

I felt delighted when_____ occurred

I love _____

Gratitude   for   _____   made   me   feel

_____

I .... _____

Chapter 2

JUDGMENT DAY

*When we realize the impermanence of our emotions and
thoughts, we can overcome them.*

~ Shubhraji

I have always been super sensitive to what the people around
me were feeling, checking in with my aunts, uncles, co-work-
ers, friends, and acquaintances in good times and when they
were dealing with a life challenge. Their pleasures and pains
became a part of my inner callings as a nurturer by nature.

When my oldest child, Amanda, was a toddler, I enrolled her
in a playgroup that consisted mostly of girls. While the children played and snacked on Cheerios, we moms chatted over
coffee, tea, fruit, and mini muffins, keeping a watchful eye.
One day, Ross, a beautiful boy with glowing blue eyes and
light brown hair, climbed onto the coffee table. I noticed some
moms rolling their eyes and complaining in hushed voices
about his boisterous, mischievous ways. His mother attempted
to intervene, but his behavior visibly upset her. *Was the child's
behavior a reflection of parenting, or was it simply his nature to explore*

while he learned to express himself? I later learned that boys tend to learn to talk later than girls. In the gossip, I remained silent. I put myself in Ross's mother's shoes. I too might one day have a rambunctious, obstinate son. If so, I wouldn't want my child's behavior complained about behind my back. That moment, when I decided I wouldn't add to the negative mom talk, was a simple but monumental one in my life.

Years later, I observed a friend making up a story about why she didn't invite another friend and child to her house. I stood by her side as she made the call, heard the little white lie, and shivered knowing it could have been me at the other end of the receiver.

As women, mothers, and friends, we are not obligated nor expected to be invited to every event or gathering planned by a host. Inner circles may shift as we interact within our families, communities, and neighborhoods. Our children's friends change, like when we were younger, as do our adult relationships. My point here is regarding those little white lies – and talk behind another's back. When we break the integrity code, we are not diminishing their shine but our own.

Men and women tend to gossip when they're bored or insecure. I don't want to generalize or offend anyone. Still, from my experience, women who have been betrayed or insulted by someone they trusted, be it a family member, friend, teacher, boss, institution, or stranger, tend to carry their emotional wounds with them. The unresolved pain can fuel insecurity or lead to unhealthy comparisons. No matter how superb our lives look, we project our issues onto others if we neglect to tend to our past. Gossip deflates.

Women wear many hats – as friends, caregivers, nurses, therapists, doctors, teachers, moms (to humans and pets), advocates, athletes, daughters, explorers, coaches, sisters, artists, actors, musicians, singers, spiritual gurus, wise women, creatives, and so on. We are powerful, beautiful, and awesome. Why, then, do we constantly feel underappreciated or unqualified?

Self-study (*Svadhyaya in Sanskrit*) cradled contemplation, offering an offset from mundane to self-aware. With support from ancient texts and spiritual offerings, we become better equipped to guide ourselves through life's perpetual phases. One of *Patanjali's sutras* (threaded pearls of wisdom) reminds us to refrain from gossip – to investigate ourselves instead of putting someone down, treating others as we would want them to treat us.

When my mind spiraled, I searched for answers. I meditated; I became a yoga teacher. Hung out with like-minded communities and circles (mostly of women). Built a conscious dome to shield myself from disruptive behaviors.

Vying for attention, approval, or love from others might be the culprit robbing women of their true shine.

I went from cheerful pigtails to ponytails, wore neon aerobics outfits (I know, so '80s!) to leather miniskirts with big hair dancing at toga parties. I shopped for vintage bags and went clubbing in New York City.

Building a breathable internal landscape before striving
to appear all put together may have made
all the difference for me back then.

When my friend's mom was ill, I changed her newborn daughter's diapers as if she were my own. I also checked in on her nuts-and-bolts project while she and her husband built their home.

Observing her and other friends struggling to keep their ailing relative alive, I feel compelled to uplift their spirits and ease their sadness.

When another friend broke her engagement, I shuffled my plans for our long-distance conversations.

After a few close friends lost their babies around the five-month mark, I reached out to them, sending notes and making phone calls to show my support.

Two dear friends had early strokes. Thankfully they both recovered, after giving many a real scare.

Another had a hysterectomy after having her first child. I knew she and her husband wanted to grow their family. Sometimes life doesn't go as planned.

Our dear friend's only child died from a brain tumor, as did the youngest son from a family in our small town. My heart ached for the unimaginable.

Friends, family, acquaintances, and yoga students suffered through treatments or lost their lives from heart attacks, breast and other forms of cancer, addiction, physical and mental health crises; others were traumatized by medical scares.

To offer comfort, I invoked radiance. I reached out in hopes of lessening their pain.

My sensitivity gave me the foresight to relate to others' feelings naturally. However, constant extensive giving to friends and family, when added to the stressors as a busy mom, had me feeling run down. It's not that the giving wasn't well received; it's just that rather than loving myself first by finding a passion or hobby, I was available for everyone whenever they called, and this corralled me into being overwhelmed.

No matter what was happening, I went out of my way to ease another. The quandary: being a nurturer without nurturing myself eroded my peace. Striving to be a good person was my attempt to put a Band-Aid on my wounds. *Why are women so quick to help others before dealing with their inner landscape? There had to be a better way, but what was it?*

Some of my carefreeness – and aspirations – slowly disappeared as I went about living.

I had to pick myself up and stop being so hard on myself. Yoga and personal development workshop tools aided me in disconnecting from expectations and judgment, replacing them with self-reliance and self-care. Meditation practices enabled me to chisel my internal Self and uncover new regions of my zone of genius. As my intuitive mind strengthened, I embraced inner peace and unleashed my creative side. Accessing *Ananda* (Sanskrit for bliss) further ignited my jovial spirit, even when life attempted (sometimes successfully) to trip me up. One example is dropping whatever I was doing to help someone else; another is finding myself within judgment's malicious grip. Either will take The Radiant Woman's ace game away. Turning a blank eye to what's right or repeating the ignorant actions of the past has the ricochet effect.

Many women (me included) think we're righteous, honest people with sincere intentions and supportive of organizations that matter to us – and perhaps we are. Yet we find ourselves judging others when in cliques or – worse – holding onto grudges or resentment. Reversing judgment requires self-love.

A radiant woman takes care of herself along with everyone else.

She's willing to go all-in by moving through her emotions and what's beneath her skin, shedding tears, releasing physical and mental pain, and beginning each day anew. By taking short, guided pauses, she has the potential to alter her karmic path.

Finding true meaning in life begins with activating spiritual bliss through cosmic connections instead of judgment and being our worst critic. Experiencing grace and joy, even during life's ups and downs, begins to feel dreamy if we choose to filter out the haze in our mind and of the world.

> Gravitating toward easing another's pain,
> That caregiving part of us remains.
> Culminating with a purpose to thrive,
> Staying positive, even when obstacles arrive.
> Steadfast love – a heart's home,
> Releasing fear of the unknown.
> Nourishing your relationship connection,
> An abacus's precise direction.

The first *yama* (or ethical rule of the yogic philosophy) is *ahimsa,* or non-violence in our actions, thoughts, and speech. Who hasn't experienced the sharp knife of words?

From children's playground taunts to grown-ups' sarcasm or demeaning equivalent, being skillful (or not) with our words can make a world of difference in how we impact our relationships. When we break the hook of habits not serving us, we revise our karma from "What goes around comes around" to dispersing our future direction projections. Shifting energetically from our temperamental mind's desires to our heart's intentions depends on us. Gossip may seem harmless because it occurs on the sidelines rather than as a direct hit, but it is still harmful to limit, judge, or speak ill of another.

The radiant woman steers from malice in conversations, chooses nonviolence in her mind, and speaks with kindness.

Our world opens with extraordinary beauty when we change our views about ourselves.

It is no small feat to shed our skin and let our true colors shine, especially when we are insecure about something in our own life. Humans want to be seen and loved, and when we accentuate their awesomeness instead of pointing out their frailties, we gain friendship, trust, and positive rapport.

Talking behind someone's back stings them, but once the words roll off our lips, we get stung too.

The venom from saying, "I'm not good enough, she has a better figure than me – oh, and by the way, she's weird," reverts to us. It turns what could have been a beautiful day into Judgment Day.

When discernment deflects venom before it morphs into unregulated thoughts and words, we feel, look, speak, and resemble our original perfection.

Where Do Internal Mistruths Come From?

Dialogue with an older relative, parent, sibling, bully, teacher, coach, or someone else we respected in which they knocked us down and gave us a reason to ditch a passion or dream.

We continue to carry old burdens, like when we saw a higher leap in dance class and thought, *She's better than me.* Why not rewrite history to sweep us towards a happier state?

Pause to rewind from decline.

External Perfection Doesn't Exist (So We Must Acquit).

Why not end the cycle, work on what we can refine within ourselves, and wipe away our mind's smog? Let go of our inner critic and naysayer by accessing our brilliant light and allowing it to shine – in person or on any virtual platform? Give ourselves energetic breathing room?

Accept the challenge to let go of those partners in crime: judgment and perfectionism. When others initiate gossip, diffuse it by redirecting conversations (e.g., to the weather). The Radiant Woman goes with the flow, be it on her yoga mat or in sports-aligned fitness classes, tennis courts, or ski slopes, to reduce insecurity, blame, and shame. She upgrades her coping skills by adapting to constant changes and taking responsible action to reflect on her belief systems.

She remains quiet or politely excuses herself to disengage from any temptation to gossip at dinner tables by:

Diverting controversial or gossip conversation (as gracefully as possible) from one subject to another.

- Pause with silence before you respond.
- Stop a thought or conversation midstream and u y again.

Disconnecting from struggles, stress, anxiety, confusion, and disappointment, can lead us to our next-level journeys. We can explore our supreme values more deeply by excelling in soul-to-soul connections.

Choosing intimate connections by sharing details about daily life's challenges to select women who support our dreams and visions. Praying for others to get through their tough times, doing good deeds respectful of nature and all people.

The Radiant Woman's Way

How to defeat the "not good enough" complex.

Challenge yourself to remain nonreactive by becoming a catalyst for love.

Contribute to your cellular health.

Catch yourself before you slip off the conscious communication path.

Reprogram Your Subconscious Mind

This can be achieved by becoming more self-aware and redefining your purpose.

* Mudra (hand position) to connect to your true nature:
  Cross index and middle finger on both hands.

Bonus: while crossing, touch your thumb to the ring finger.

Eyes open or closed.

Take this hand gesture on-the-go or sit in a chair or cushion on the floor.

Hold for 1 to 3 minutes while taking long, deep breaths.

* Mudra Variation: Connect the thumb and ring finger to signal pure thoughts for clear communication.

Hand gestures are a formula for your shine. They encourage you to lend a helping hand without feeling depleted, the Radiant Woman's Way!

Chapter 3

FORGIVE AND ACCEPT

*"May we embrace the highest aspect of
who we truly are. LOVE."*

~ Seane Corn

Though my devoted husband took out the trash, helped with dishes, and happily provided our family with a beautiful home and lifestyle, I blamed him on occasion when I felt alone. Those thoughts started soon after our first little one was born. I didn't know it then, but my lack of direction, except for taking care of my family, left my mind, at times, wandering in the *wrong* direction.

While making recipes for friends and family to enjoy, in between nursing a baby and juggling the rest of the house, my internal world kept shifting from happy one moment to wanting Jonathan's attention the next.

As he completed tasks, sat proudly on his lime green and yellow John Deere lawn mower after a day of work in New York

City, I felt surges of built-up resentment. *If only I had my own passion project and could escape to the great outdoors like he did!*

I craved a realistic outlet for when feelings of overwhelm and tiredness settled in my body.

Thinking about what I did wrong constantly overshadowed my spirit. Unspoken relationship doubts sprouted in my mind. *Was he sneaking off with a lover when I was "too tired" or not feeling well in mind, body, and spirit…or at least fantasizing about it?*

Later, as our children grew into young adults, other questions arose. *What will our lives look like when it's just us? Were we meant to be?* Many women I have spoken to have asked themselves the same thing. I am thankful I chose to grow emotionally and spiritually and that our love connection has grown deeper too.

Hubby once said, "I'm not a mind-reader," adding that he was there for me. So why had I projected mistruths or made-up stories in my head?

The ancient wisdom practices I explored on and off my yoga mat began to dissolve misconceptions and contrived blame and shame. It happened organically as I worked to develop my strengths and passions so that I too could be independent and rediscover the premarital me.

Then, after the epiphany about giving my power away *long before* we got hitched, I strove to resolve incomplete work related to my childhood desires and relationships.

As I relied on myself for love, I accepted love from my parents and husband without expectations. Renewing vows to make amends creates healthier environments for relationships to flourish. When we forgive, we bring closure, bridge families' hope to repair, and start anew. May each woman, parent, child, and teacher honor life as a practice. We, like our parents, come into this world with open wounds. If we tend to them as they come, emotions can move and won't get stuck. Acknowledging and processing our emotions, even if they are painful, is healthier than avoiding them. Human beings are simultaneously experiencing and creating their history. When we use conscious communication by relating to others, finding something in common with another person, and remembering they too were once a child, we can clear the path for improved relations.

If we want to find true radiance and stop the resentment factor, we surrender to love instead of the need to be correct.

The Radiant Woman embraces forgiveness
for her freedom's sake by realizing that nobody's
opinion defines her.

The Radiant Woman's signature way to play is forgiveness for what he, she, or they said (or didn't say) by noticing the good stuff and repelling the ambiguity.

I tried and implemented new, self-approved conversations with myself by observing my thoughts instead of attending to my mindless voice. I delved deep into my emotional baggage, rather than staying on the surface. The rinsing process of purification encouraged me to gain peace as an adjunct to forgiveness, freedom, and relief.

The Radiant Woman leaves her mark gently, softly, and powerfully without diminishing anyone else's shine. She understands or is willing to forgo being right because, in the end, the only one she can count on is herself. She doesn't look to a partner or friend to complete herself.

Women need to insert compassion for all beings into their current relationships. Injecting tender, loving kindness brings us closer to radiance.

As I lunged my body with arms high or stretched over, lengthening them on my mat, I listened to my teachers' words, felt them running through me. I channeled their energy, built thousands of years ago, to the current time. I applied transforming life principles to my own life. In becoming, I accepted my birth family with compassion. I wanted others – my friends, family, and the world – to know love as I had found it. Unbeknownst to me, self-love gave me new eyes to view life, and I wanted to share it with others so they, too, could find acceptance and move on to what mattered most: peace of mind.

In its purest form, yoga is a mystical aspect of the Hindu culture, steeped in Eastern traditions, rituals, and meditative concepts. God, or the higher universal power associated with any religion or belief system, can be located within oneself. The Radiant Woman invites her teacher within to renew her faith. Yoga, meditation, and walking in nature led me to investigate *Kabbalah,* or Jewish mysticism, online with my temple during the pandemic.

Its foundational text invites us to experience our spiritual selves as a metaphor for Jacob's climb.

Prayer is the ladder that helps us ascend from our earthly existence to a higher state of consciousness. It leads us to the divine essence within us. I plan to study and better understand my consciousness from its teachings again.

Since the beginning, people have stood on ceremony for what they believed in, guided by popular opinion or principle. When they return to loving themselves through awareness and consider the concept of Godliness or a higher source of energy, their attentive love and devotion can be felt by others. By embracing one's spiritual side, we can lift ourselves up and subsequently lift those around us as well.

One day, acclaimed author Harlan Coben's yoga mat was next to mine as I jotted notes from the teacher in my journal. Later, he turned to me and said, "Isn't learning wasted on the youth?" Recalling those required academic years as a youngster and young adult, I often felt obligated to pursue book learning without a strong sense of purpose. Whether it was for standardized tests or researching subjects that didn't interest me, it all felt like a waste of time. I would have much rather been on the beach or hanging out with friends. That experience contrasts sharply with the new me, now filled with spiritual and self-aware curiosity. No longer confined to sitting behind a desk with a number-two pencil, competing with my peers, I've discovered a more fulfilling path. My mind feels content and alive as I devour wise words offering introspection, and my spirit feels wholesome and vibrant when flowing through yoga classes. Those past days pale in comparison to the sense of connection and purpose I now experience. "So true," I replied, "I love being a student of life now. I didn't back then."

Certain foods restore gut health to alkaline (rather than acidity), revving our metabolism and inducing sparkle. I often begin my day with warm lime, salt, and ginger. I also boil a cut-up apple with cinnamon sticks (noted for its pungent, sweet taste, and bitter properties, heat activating) beneficial for digestion. Next, adding cloves alleviates my irritable bowel / leaky gut symptoms. This is a perfect recipe for detoxing if you overeat or indulge in foods that aggravate your stomach.

I learned this remedy from Ayurvedic Master Chef/Healer Sheryl Edsall: " It helps the digestive fire start in the morning. It is soothing for the stomach and excellent for your skin."

For recipe:

> 1 apple
> 4 whole cloves (Full of antioxidants, they help your body fight free radicals, which damage your cells. They are good for your mind and purify your blood.)
> A few cinnamon sticks
> Vanilla (optional)
> Peel the apple if it's not organic. Also, consider this support regimen as seasonal (when apples taste better).

Accelerating the use of the six tastes in food choices and cooking can replace sugar and alcohol and add pep to our steps. According to Ayurveda (the sister science to yoga), combining the six tastes (salt, sweet, bitter, spicy/pungent, sour, and astringent) in our meals makes us feel more satisfied and helps us digest our food more easily.

We can improve our health by focusing on nature's inherent ability to grow, repair, and rebuild through changing seasons, life cycles, and even after storms or natural disasters. We can also harness the power of visualization, imagining vibrant green fields alongside golden koi fish, symbolizing the resilience and flow of life. Nature operates through a multitude of interconnected forces, from brightly colored dahlias and lilac bouquets to the cycles of the animal food chain and the process of natural decay. The sun rises and sets, yet the lotus remains unscathed, blooming with serene illumination from the murky waters.

Anyone seeking personal revelations can allocate time to soak in our brilliant world beyond the horizon. listening to soulful vibrations cues wise women to remember who they are. Stress leaves us clues. Resentment can take years off our lives. Expecting someone who "did us wrong" to pay the price is as dangerous as ingesting toxins. Forgiveness is not about the other person. We reap a sweeter life when we rise above the bitter chatter and auto-repeat stories.

Meditation primes our minds for conducive interplay, flooding us with insightful, refreshing outlooks.

One myth I enjoy debunking is that you must sit silently (cave-like dwelling) to meditate or bend like a pretzel to practice yoga. On the contrary, yoga and meditation come in many physical and abstract forms. Escaping modern living and reconnecting with nature and our bodies brings happiness. There's no denying it – nature has a way of transforming our lives. From gaining a sense of peace to helping us find true happiness, connecting to our heart centers and with the great outdoors can profoundly impact us all.

Surrendering and accepting what is – by dissolving recurring conflicts within ourselves in bite-size increments – permits us to pause, rewrite our stories, and replace patterns without attachment to others' actions. The seeker who places her intention on transformation puts herself in a solid position to access a peaceful state.

Letting breath awareness guide our imagination, using sensory stimuli to release stress, enables mindful living.

Working through unfinished emotional business by releasing past wounds and using them for our greatest good opens us to channel radiance.

Removing mental obstacles (for example, by cutting through strands of fragmented relationships) further increases the manifestation process. Changing our breath flow accelerates the redirection of negative thoughts to positive ones as the oxygen regenerates. Connecting to what's important to you through acts of forgiveness frees you to receive love, peace, and light – speaking with kindness to yourself (and in return, sharing your heart, from your soul, with others). The process encourages resolving a severed relationship.

The Radiant Woman's Way

As per Dr. Hew Len, *Ho'oponopono,* a Hawaiian healing modality introduced to me in a forgiveness workshop with Shubhraji, translates to "make things right."

In this four-step process, the participant tries to rid themselves of burdensome thoughts and teaches the importance of love and forgiveness.

The shift happens and lasts if we continue to rearrange the narrative and welcome modifications with no expectations.

Anything is possible when we come from our hearts and not our heads.

To begin, think of a relationship we want to heal or transform. The person can be living or in the spirit world.

Write this out then say it aloud:

1. *I'm Sorry* – admit personal responsibility to enhance relationship healing

2. *I love you* – with meaning and conviction

3. *Please forgive me* – for the things I said, did, and or didn't act on

4. *Thank you* – with gratitude for the lessons learned (not easy at all to see when you're in the heat of turmoil or the situation has been engrained with pain for a long time). This process can be repeated often and soften your reactive mind with the grace of time.

Repeatedly say thank you to this being for your human connection.

If you're face-to-face with the person, practice for five minutes. Think about your thoughts and feelings and express them to your partner with real feelings.

Releasing blame permits us to repair and progress in our relationships, The Radiant Woman's Way.

Chapter 4

LOOK AT LIFE LIKE
A BROADWAY SHOW

*"We need to expose our true selves and let go of the
filters – because that's real, that's authentic,
and that's beautiful."*

~ Katie Sands

I recall one hot summer night when the crickets chirped and fireflies sparked, I felt like I was barely keeping my head above water. The overwhelm was becoming increasingly, well, overwhelming. Looking back, the persistent rashes flaring up on my abdomen were attempting to encourage me to change.

If I had known it was up to me to save myself from worry, I might have wasted less time in fear and adjusted my time for developing and rediscovering my creative potential sooner.

The constant coming and going within our family unit matched the likes of a marching band parading at a football game. Synchronized noise permeated our walls and floorboards with hustle and bustle. In addition to pitter-pattering foot-steps and the revolving kitchen, another sound bubbled over into our flowing orchestra of life. Aquarium sump pumps droned, and though impressive, each hissing sound made by this tubular apparatus felt strange to me – a newer instal-lation percolated into fruition when we reconfigured our kitchen. Hubby's hobby – a mysterious underworld of *Little Nemos*, colorful striped wrasse, and exotics dancing amongst slippery anemones, sand, and coral reefs – soon expanded from our kitchen to the basement. It was an ever-present science experiment for gawking children and visitors, from maintaining the tanks and chillers for optimal temperature to meticulously preventing algae overgrowth and treating virus outbreaks.

Sometimes, when I was cooking or lost in thought, the marine life would muffle my hearing when someone asked me a question. I noticed my nervous system was sensitive to the structures.

Inadvertently, I discovered a sense of harmony in the noise.

One day, as I sat alone long after the children left for school, I drew my chair close to one tank. Feeling captivated by its soothing quality while sipping tea, my body relaxed into a trance-like, meditative state.

What if the tank's humming taught me a lesson on adjusting my mind's temperament as it fluctuated? What was I not hearing based on my current sensitivity or mood? As I leaned into the bub-bling water flow, I repelled distractions. Drifted into opulent presence.

Calming breath practices, infused with mantras, brought peace to my imbalanced life; they allowed me to focus my thoughts and repurpose extraneous energy. I observed all inner and outside noise when I, along with my family and friends, connected to our devices. Conscious thinking became non-existent in the influx of mobile phones, personal computers, and big-screen TVs. All simple and complex technological factors were here to stay. Since electrical surges drained me, I considered infrastructure counterbalances around me for optimal mental health alignment. Utilizing the elements of earth, fire, water, wind, and air to counterbalance our mood attunes our altered center. There are also things like adorning your body with a necklace or bracelet made of copper – a material noted for its shielding properties and protection from electromagnetic fields (EMF radiation) that come from devices.

Life's constant fluctuation became apparent as I observed the output generated by objects and those around me as if it were a movie screen. Just like movie popcorn, the buttery overflow ran its course. Our "problems" might not disappear overnight, but by noticing our situational settings coming and going like any snack time or meal, we train our minds to be less reactive when "blah-blah" happens.

At times, Hubby's noise-producing hobbies and gadgets – from big boy toys that go vroom, vroom to remote controls (why are there so many channels and clickers?) – irked me. *Then I remembered that staying centered if/when I felt off-balance was up to me. Plus, who was I to pass judgment on his hobbies when I had a few of my own?*

The peculiar sounds from my harmonium, with its repetitive mantras, and the Eastern music I played might not appeal to others. Some like it hot, some like it not – be it hip hop or rock music, evening wear or athleisure, everyday handbags to Gucci clutches, etc.

The excess items in my life occupied valuable space, indirectly cluttering my mind. Different-sized jeans and bras were stored underneath my wearable clothes, adding to the chaos. *Feng Shui* experts and organizers say if we haven't worn the item in a long while, it's time to detach and release it. Although the concept is agreeable, some may need to cultivate the skill of implementation.

Non-attachment to material objects and mind clutter is a big part of yogic teachings. From outside sources to inside factors, stripping away what's no longer needed brings a return to our equilibrium.

The Radiant Woman understands the importance of self-awareness and chooses to uncover her true essence to feel.

Even in excess, dinner chatter was the exception to the rule. Sharing stories and laughing together during mealtimes was the deliciousness I craved, especially during the quarantine. Covid allowed many of us to moderate our tendencies and reevaluate our relationships with unprecedented astuteness. Many of us were forced to work through fears of the unknown. And, as we visited our emotions, we might have noticed some of our hand-me-downs – or ancestral baggage that had infiltrated our families and perpetuated conditioning.

It was now up to us to strip our emotional ownership of these outdated models and root systems while maintaining valuable assets like relationships. Being disturbed enough to change led me into silence, listening to my breath's finely-tuned sound notes in an intimate meditation setting. And because I felt so great after days, hours, or mini-moment pauses, taking time for myself took on an ulterior motive.

Science has proven that the "high" we feel after achieving or receiving an object or goal doesn't last long. Explorative cycles crave counterbalanced activity, as do structured perspectives. Being in nature, no matter where we are in our day, can help keep our goals in check.

Denim and yoga pants are my preferred staples. Dressing up with party shoes has its percolating effects too. Putting on makeup has a meditative quality I liken to my passion for artistic expression and painting on a clean canvas. Accessorizing our life with celebrations, frivolities, and collectibles has its place. Purchasing gifts for people we care about can bring us immense joy and satisfaction.

Buzzing Sounds

As I paid closer attention to what was in front of me through loving eyes, I appreciated the protein enzyme fish aquariums with their cosmetic displays. Adjusting my inner voice sounds invoked me and allowed me to filter out noisy conversations in my head.

Not everyone overthinks.

When we take responsibility for our thought-provoking actions, give purpose to being of service to others, and release external blame for situational behaviors that are not ours to mandate, we can collectively improve human relations. This type of admission can be achieved even when one side of a partnership surrenders for the greatest good.

We can build new infrastructures within our body to support our immune system, alleviate pressurized thoughts, boost gut health, and revamp our hardwired minds to be content and satiated with sacred correspondence. Each sensitivity can move us into a deep respect for our natural connections as humans. It is widely known that there are robots powered by artificial intelligence (AI) that can perform tasks much faster than humans can. While AI can be highly efficient, it cannot replace the personal touch that comes from human interaction. A handwritten note tailored to the individual can go a long way in establishing a meaningful connection. A generation of students no longer write by hand. What is the cost of losing this skill? My first business mentor, Sarah Walton said it this way: "Our phones are 'weapons of mass distraction,' and if you want to find something out (before calling a more tech-savvy youth) why not 'GTS it' (Google That S---) because that's what they're gonna do and it's how to learn for ourselves."

Animals and forests grow with sequential decay from sequoias, oaks, and elms. As today's devices prevent social engagement and AI emotes a lack of heartfelt emotions, we are being led back to nature to bathe in forests. Plus, there's no substitution for a serene lake or a Japanese maple maroon leaf tree to instill inner calm.

The Radiant Woman's Way

Breath awareness meditations can be practiced while walking, reclining, or sitting.

Mindful Minute Pauses for Self-Attunement

- Give yourself a nourishing facial reflexology massage. Each time you move your hands onto specific pressure points, you improve your circulation by gently enhancing the skin's metabolism while relaxing strained, tired, and tense facial muscles.
- Bring your forefinger and middle finger of each hand to your temples.
- Rub your fingers in a circular massage motion (this is a beautiful give-and-receive tool to share).
- Trace fingers under the eye on the cheekbone outward.
- Pinch under the chin to ears.
- Pull down on ears.
- Stretch your jaw to release facial tension (open your mouth wide and close it a few times).
- Dry scalp revival: Massage your scalp with your fingertips, then gently pull from the roots.

Here's a 4-7-8 Breath Count

- If you're having trouble falling asleep or feel anxious, counting from four to seven to eight is an effective method.

- Close your eyes or let a little light in.
- Inhale one, two, three, four.
- Hold your breath one, two, three, four, five, six, seven.
- Exhale one, two, three, four, five, six, seven, eight.
- You can start your practice for one, three, or five minutes, gradually building up on time.

(When one sense turns off, we heighten another by creating an inner connection to ourselves.)

This applicable tool can positively influence your sensory system. Keep pausing, breathing and counting. Meditation is as simple as that!

Chapter 5

CONSCIOUS CONNECTIONS NOT ONLY CREATE RELATIONS; THEY DEFINE THEM.

"Love is like a beautiful flower which I may not touch,
but whose fragrance makes the garden a place of delight
just the same."

~ Helen Keller

At a tender time when my social life meant everything to me, my mom and dad set some rules. Mopeds were off limits, deemed unsafe forms of transportation. Like many teenagers, I looked to my peers for outward acceptance and attention. I also had a streak of rebelliousness that tested my parents' limits.

One Saturday night, I was grounded for coming home past my 11:00 p.m. curfew the previous weekend. Looking back, I must have frightened my parents by acting from my ego and underdeveloped mind. Little did they know I was already planning to cross those boundaries again.

As they prepared for bed, I climbed out my third-story attic bedroom window via a fire escape ladder – my destination: a peer's party. After landing safely, I walked downhill from my house and trekked a few miles to the party. I wasn't there long before my parents discovered me missing. I'm sure they were quite disappointed with my behavior. Dad drove to the place I thought mattered most and called me out.

Fortunately, I had other, less rebellious outlets to help me release teenage emotions – from weekly jazz classes to playing lacrosse, the latter a new program for us girls. Then I discovered a non-athletic activity that brought out the best in me.

My mom opened Beadazzles, an exclusive boutique where mothers, daughters, sisters, grandmas, and friends could feel pampered and creative. Faux, flashy, big, and chunky were all the rage in 1982. Amongst the glitz and glamor, I was in my element. Beading jewelry became a catalyst that helped shape me into the person I am today.

Like many, teenage drama and typical hormonal shifts governed my life. Thankfully, I found an artistic escape to separate from my peers and work on my craft after school and on weekends. Although I didn't realize it then, this job allowed my inner creativity to bloom. Standing behind the glass showcases, I felt alive. Communicating with customers enabled me to make suggestions and influence their decisions through personal selling. Some of us who worked at the store also brought the Beadazzles experience to other jewelry-making events. Kids' beading parties, where they had the opportunity to string tiny black and white plastic initials for their names and colored flower bead bracelets/necklaces, were especially rewarding.

At Beadazzles, displays held separate clear cups filled with freshwater pearls, lapis, corals, turquoise, black onyx, tiger's eye, amethyst, mother-of-pearl, and other semi-precious stones. Customers browsed, created, or purchased ready-made jewelry with dangling trinkets and semi-precious gems.

Each customer who walked through those double glass doors could choose from the existing jewelry pieces and accessories, including studded belts, bags, and other rhinestone-covered merchandise. They could also design jewelry with a sales assistant, then craft their masterpiece independently or have us string the beads for them.

Arranging beads in a pattern or stringing them randomly on a wire brought a look of delight to their faces. The creative atmosphere resulted in high energy for all. Certain customers hung out long after their purchase to spend time with Mom, me, and the other salespeople. Small talk often led to deeper conversations about life's "under the sun" topics. For the most part, my brother and father were not a part of the "club," but we welcomed our friend Robert Verdi, a regular *schmoozer* (Yiddish for "talker" or "charmer") who added to any conversation related to fanciful, flashy fashion.

Customers and staff alike held Mom's opinion in high regard. She provided valuable advice on topics ranging from fashion to relationships. I'm thankful to have gained respect for my mother beyond our home by observing her as a female boss.

Attending the New York Gift Show (which was held at the Jacob Javits Center and featured home and fashion accessories from various designers) as a "buyer" representing "the store" empowered me. We selected wholesale pre-made products with the hope that they would be well-received by the end user. Beadazzles journeyed during one of the hottest fashion trends of the 1980s.

I especially loved the adrenaline rush when men selected last-minute gifts for their girlfriends, daughters, or wives on Christmas Eve and Valentine's Day.

Some customers were harder to satisfy, while others boasted about how well their gifts were received. The customizable wearable art experience turned many into raving, loyal fans.

Their appreciative feedback made us, the staff behind the counter, smile too. Friendliness, along with a colorful environment, fostered great camaraderie. From what I remember, Mom seemed happy. She had an outlet for herself. It gave me and my siblings time to fend for our independence. Her entrepreneurship came at a poignant time in my life.

What we think about ourselves can either carve out pathways for greatness or defeat us as we set out into our unknown futures.

Threading beads had its hidden therapeutic benefit. Designing kept me in passion mode and away from personal drama. With great fortune, it also filled my bank account with spending money and my first taste of financial freedom.

I contributed to the business for ten-plus years as a daughter and employee.

While in college, I gathered supplies from the shop and assembled my crafts there. Though it took courage to start "Marla's Creations" on campus, the side gig came naturally to me.

It also provided additional spending money with flexible working hours. I'd set up my vending table in the student union, sorority houses, and dorm rooms, displaying original and other designer pieces.

Being of service, hugging each other, and using our hands weaves us together. Kindness, while maintaining an imaginative curiosity, sharpens our minds.

After Bedazzles' closure, the fashion trends shifted towards traditional looks featuring pearls and stones set in gold and silver. It was just as well that the chapter ended because Mom shifted into her next role as a supportive, hands-on grandma. My father often said, "There's nothing like becoming a grandparent. At the end of the day, if the kids cry, we pass them back to their parents!"

My sister Abby, five years younger than me, has always had an artistic flair. Though we overlapped while working at Mom's store, our bond with beads came after. She created a unique, dazzling, stylized, down-to-earth jewelry line when she was on campus and later launched "How Charming." I admired her drive, designs, and postcard announcements she created for wholesale event sales in Manhattan and at my home.

Abby's collection was splayed on our dining room table for consecutive-day sales. This was when my beading skills reemerged. I added clasps to some pieces and was delighted to offer a helping hand of service. In addition to selling and interacting with customers, I enhanced her inventory by purchasing unusual items including cashmere scarves, bamboo wraps, candles, frames, and hair ties. As the gourmet hostess, I also baked, served tea, muffins, and fruit, veggies, and dips to fuel shoppers.

Women still rave about Abby's charming merchandise and witty presence.

For all beings, especially women crafters, quilters, beaders, clay potters, sewers, knitters, and so on, keeping those age-old skills alive for the next generation is vital. It has a therapeutic effect, and when you craft with someone in mind, it is infused with the intention for them to adorn themselves. Also, when you get into a passion zone, you're meditative. The value of these kinds of skills became apparent during the pandemic.

Realization

Nowadays, teens contend with socialization deficits caused by social media, which doesn't replace reality. Life was tough enough before this instant gratification of destructive clicks came into play. Hiding behind keyboards and screens allows us to avoid emotions and go numb with a scroll's touch. Managing those emotions in today's social scene adds additional layers for all ages.

Staying connected to our grammar, high school, and college friends – and people in all phases of our lives – has become instant. Before social media, I prioritized staying connected to my networks in celebration and during challenges.

Many of us are regaining long-lost friends celebrating their milestones from afar. When a kindergarten friend I'd lost touch with reached out via Facebook, we reminisced. Social media brings people together, but it also pulls our relations apart. Emotional touchpoints present an entirely new series of life pressures. Navigating tomorrow's unprecedented future requires both online platforms and in-person interactions. Human attention is in an all-new dimension.

Uniting with people who share similar interests in *kula* (community) spaces supports us in our higher selves; their energy alleviates opposition in the world. I love it when women cheerlead each other, celebrate each other's accomplishments, give out beautiful compliments, and find a threaded connection through sharing our stories and listening. Bridging communication gaps in personal and business partnerships requires tenacious effort.

If our inner critic attempts to zap our powerful energy, we rearrange our thoughts. Replacing them with new ones before they get the best of us sweeps angst away. Finding supportive outlets helps us tap into our genius muses. Releasing attachment to yesterday ensures a brighter and perhaps even enlightened future.

Recently, I laughed with friends upon reading excerpts from our friend Jen's high school diaries. In it, she wrote of our fears and boy crush dreams. Kudos go to Debbie, our senior class president, who remembers details as if it were yesterday. Shifts happen when we write, talk, laugh, create, or move our bodies with intent!

Isn't testing the waters a rite of passage for all of us as we grow up?

Navigating uncertainty and shifting to virtual learning during the pandemic brought us new baggage. Many lost their independence, and peers' lack of connections dramatically affected their psyches.

Whether from childhood or yesterday, wounds carry over if we do not resolve old patterns or learned behaviors. Our internal thoughts either positively influence our character or undermine our brilliance.

The Radiant Woman's Way

Feeling down? Try taking a new route to your favorite coffee shop.

Talk with anyone, ask questions, engage with strangers and people you barely know, and smile to contribute to another person's day positively.

The Magic of Inner Peace

Changing our attitudes with movement leads us to shine from one transition to another.

Cross-Body Stretch Sequence to balance your brain's left and right hemispheres, resolve a past emotion, and get out of your comfort zone by creating change.

- Bring your hands out wide.
- Cross them with a hug in front of your heart.
- Bring your hands out wide.
- Cross them with a hug in front of your heart, this time with the other arm on top.
- Continue alternating your hugging motion until you feel complete.
- Hold your self-love hug as long as it feels good.
- With arms still crossed, squeeze your upper arms, walking hands up and down your arms.
- Next, reach your arms wide again, then cross them, placing the opposite fingers under your armpits with thumbs pressed in front.

- Close your eyes (if you are comfortable doing so or in a quieter setting).
- Shrug shoulders high (giving yourself an awkward hug).
- Press elbows down toward the side of the chest.
- Inhale and exhale in a full breath from the lower aspect of the lung to its upper region so your belly and chest can rise and relax.
- Embrace the armpit crossed position even if it does not feel comfortable.
- Hang in there for 1-3 minutes (otherwise visualize).
- To end, inhale, hold your breath, and squeeze the arm position along with your entire body from nose to toes.
- Exhale by shaking your arms and hands.
- Rest your hands like a basket in your lap, breathing long and deep.
- Pause to notice how you feel.

Visualization

Imagine a beautiful bouquet filled with all your favorite flowers. Begin spreading the colorful energy to all beings, even those with whom you might not see eye-to-eye. Turn on an automatic sequence by imaging sparks of loving projection.

Chapter 6

WHEN TWO LIGHT ENERGIES ATTRACT EACH OTHER

"The only person you are destined to become is the person you decide to be."

~ Ralph Waldo Emerson

What caused an intuitive, sensitive, creative Being, driven by personal ambitions, to let many of her dreams go?

I was enveloped in my husband's generous love daily. Our family's lifestyle allowed me to revolve my days around their needs.

Since Jonathan ensured our house was in working order (he scheduled a plumber or electrician when needed), I naturally fell into my full-time role of motherhood. I was laid back, even "super chill." Yet, my husband's passion for figuring things out continued as our family grew, whereas I lacked direction and value.

With our differing energies, we provided a well-rounded perspective on parenting. Being each other's teammates leveled the game. Occasional quarrels and bickering about child-rearing, family tumult outside of our core six, and what to spend money on (or not) tested our resilience. *Were our differences shattering or advancing us to grow together or apart? Were we a power couple leading in partnership? Where would he be without my support in caring for our children's physical and emotional needs and acting as a social coordinator? Could I be brazen enough to stand up for what I believed in and lovingly readminister my newfound values?*

If I wanted to get along and accept the man I loved for who he was, there had to be a better process for relating to our differences, one being his impatience. *Santosha,* a Sanskrit word meaning contentment, is the Buddha's way. I poured my heart and hands into *Shradha* (Sanskrit) and *Tikvah* (Hebrew) for faith and hope. Bounded together by trust, our marriage challenges us to be considerate of our differences.

Jonathan's disciplined strength differed from my spontaneous (as in, I don't need a plan) nature. Our partnering brought out possibilities in one another. We harnessed our passion through our love for family, adventure, and travel.

Though his strong, husky, TV-remote-holding trader voice commanded authority, my softer voice and opinions mattered. Yoga, tai chi, contemplative, thought-provoking conversation, mantra meditation, and women's groups helped me gain insight into the rootedness of human behavior.

My mission was to stand up for my beliefs and resolve without conflict. At times, I got angry and slipped. Upon self-admission and in unity with patience being a virtue, I tried to stay steady, neutral, and non-reactive. The Radiant Woman is open to discovering her shine by letting her partner move through his emotions without judgment.

Since opposites attract, being both a giver and receiver, a doer (not a moaner), and taking action to undo any personal misdoing could advance our union. Just like we danced to Michael Crawford's "That's All I Ask of You" (from Andrew Lloyd Webber's original *Phantom*) for our wedding song, and although I tried to take his lead when we took lessons, I let him lead the way to avoid collision. Wouldn't it be fantastic if children witnessed their parents' lovers quarrel through the darkness and reconcile to a common ground? When adults are willing to reconsider opposing views and work toward noticing the positives in one another, compromise, compassion, and forgiveness, the younger generations learn better communication and love.

Who was I to complain when he chose to mow the lawn himself rather than asking one of our kids to do it? Why take away his pleasure of being a great outdoorsman? Our family benefited from his labor as he was often home in the evenings and on weekends. While some men golfed eighteen rounds or hung out in bars, Jonathan worked the land just like in a greenhouse, having made soil and learned the ropes of landscaping as a teen.

He was scheduled, a jack of many trades, an ambitious man pursuing exuberance. His way of attaining goals and completing projects differed from mine. As a multi-tasker, I was quickly sidetracked, fell off balance, or lagged, whereas he stayed focused on one task at a time.

Here's one ritual that has barely changed since we met:

Weight-lifting schedule
Monday: triceps
Tuesday: legs and squats
Wednesday: pass
Thursday: biceps
Friday: legs
Weekends: weight training. This time was reserved
for family, friends, and projects around the house.

His propensity to decompartmentalize and serve by doing things his way counterbalanced my spontaneous personality. And when his opinions irritated me, I strove to love and respect him despite our differences. As I developed more substantial commitments in meditation practices, I felt grateful for his high-achieving success formula instead of feeling inept. Our magnetic force kept us connected.

Movement helps us follow our dreams instead of chasing or comparing ourselves to others. I pay the price when I am less disciplined with fitness routines since I know I feel my best with movement structure. When wakening before sunrise, I exfoliate by dry brushing my skin, rub essential oil on my footpads and under my arms, and take a cold shower before I sit to meditate. *Sadhana* (daily spiritual practices) offered a total upgrade because it was done as a lead-up to and in conjunction with movements, breathing techniques, and chanting. After assuming each posture, I sat quietly and repeated mantras before anyone, including the dog, woke up. My disciplined workouts and meditations filled me with vibrance.

Influencing and encouraging change in another is through affection, not anger. We open doors to acceptance when we respect similarities and differences in our partnerships. The ability to discern the right to our feelings, thoughts and opinions can enliven our careers and personal relations. Radiance generates positive energy. It affects those around us by creating an attitude flow meant to be shared.

Focusing on one task at a time creates a win-win success formula. Setting time limits and structure promotes ancient wisdom philosophies. It empowers instead of disempowers.

Jon's regimens gave me insight into a personal trait I yearned to cultivate.

He filled in gaps where I lacked certain skill sets, and I'd like to think some of my woo-woo ways have rubbed off on him. As my spiritual life progressed via yoga meditation and rituals, I also implemented lifestyle systems to keep me motivated and on track.

Why do partners react to each other's opposite behaviors if polarities make the world ticktock?

Suppose my husband wasn't super-communicative regarding emotional awareness but was embracing his connection to nature and people in his way. Who was I to say he was doing it wrong?

I realized his *bodhisattva* (self-assured contentment and containment) made him a high achiever. He was efficient when cooking (pancakes and barbecuing until the pandemic, when he effortlessly took on all recipes) and cleaning up in our kitchen. Was it OCD of him to line the dishwasher's forks, knives, and plates to ensure they would be super-clean? I found it amusing when he moved his placemat aside to prevent its being spilled on, only to have drips land on the table instead. Despite his compulsive, diligent, and meticulous neatness, he too often has a messy desk.

His insistence challenged me to investigate my reactive mind. It was up to me to be patient and to compromise. I flourished in his company, just as he did in mine. Plus, my softness was the perfect complement to his orderliness.

Shaking off stress to feel my best in womanhood became my number-one goal. It led me to practice intentional love through forgiveness.

My desperate yearning and questioning about who I was crystallized my pillars of strength. Realizing our constantly evolving aspirations allows us to experience a sense of self-worth. Letting go of grudges and resentments can harmonize our relationships.

Women have different love languages than men. When we learn how to navigate relationships with people of varying personalities, we become equipped to understand each other's roles as complementary and equal in partnerships. Where expectations from outward love were random, I dismantled my misconceptions − and uncovered unsettled emotions through self-awareness. Seeing the *wabi-sabi* (A Japanese context of two words to see beauty in the cracks) is a perfect stimulus for an enriched life because opposites attract, like the sun, moon, sky, and earth. (See Appendix.)

It's a choice to set boundaries – NO phone before bed or any device at the dinner table (working on it).

We don't even know what we don't know... until we're shown another way. Once we understand, if we don't act or find a new way of accepting differences, willful ignorance comes into play. Meditative states through one directed focus such as candle-gazing or counting my breath allowed me to attain extensive periods of true bliss. In return, I became attentive to our relationship by finding commonalities.

Valuable insights can be gained by recognizing and highlighting positive character qualities.

As radiant women, we remain ardently committed, as we did when we took our intimate vows to love and accept our differences in marital challenges.

One day, while on retreat, I confided in one of the other women that my husband had no interest in the "spiritual stuff."

She replied matter-of-factly, "Most people, usually women, ask their spouses for a divorce once they find spiritual freedom and bliss."

Thoughts of my best grammar school friend Jackie's parents rushed to my mind. Why had her mom asked for a divorce? They had completed construction on their dream home and moved in. Did she yearn for accomplishment beyond marriage and motherhood? To master something to invigorate her soul? Why had the life she lived no longer lived up to her expectations? Those of us with ambitions want to grow, connect to our soul's purpose, pursue our dreams and careers, learn with spatial opportunities – alongside motherhood – something that wasn't popular or accepted for women forty-plus years ago, when a void existed. Today, many couples either separate before soul-searching or remain in loveless marriages.

Hmmm, I thought to myself. Though Jon was not a spiritual man, he was a loving man. Our love and commitment to each other felt passionate and intense. He might not want to change or express his emotions like some men do, yet I'd been placed in his life for a reason. I appreciated his support and felt grateful when he bought me roses, caressed me softly, and connected his hands to nature's powerful landscapes. He put his heart and soul into our family, friends, travel, the lawn, flowers, cars, fish maintenance, and more.

He transformed his state of being, whether skiing on mountains or boogie boarding with our children in Ogunquit, Maine. Though he didn't outwardly appear meditative, his playful personality when using his hands to build and fix for our family and in life manifested naturally as extenders of his heart. He tried and often mastered anything he wanted to learn, likening it to skilled musicians and artists. His supernatural methodical rhythm flowed like a river conduit, even if he didn't "believe."

In response to the woman's comment: I wanted no part of giving up on my love connection. I wanted to influence and improve my communication skills as I improved myself.

Relationships give us reasons to thrive; they prime us for growth. We often differed, yet I felt in my bones that we were a match. Our love flowed together even when we were apart, each influencing the other for the better. We made amends when we clashed – accepted each other regardless of our differences.

It had taken us a lot to get to where we were, and I looked forward to enhancing our life together. Every step we took fostered connective depth in our relationship.

Yet, hanging over my head (ever since my father-in-law pointed it out early on in our marriage) was the statistic, "Fifty percent of all marriages lead to divorce." Since that remains true today, it is up to us to challenge the status quo. Another statistic proclaims that women usually initiate divorce. As radiant women, we can decide if we want to reformat those margins by reinitiating love instead of letting it go.

I dared to claim my power through neutrality rather than polarity. I opened my heart wider. A partnership is the merging of two lives and upbringings, where the individual at play becomes accustomed to expecting change as they question each other with compassion and require compromise to build a new entity.

My soul-searching led me to unravel my partner and see him as a separate entity. By remembering our vows, I felt more committed to validating our love for each other. May the song we cut for our wedding cake, the Archies' "Sugar, Sugar," be sweetened by each other's arms to outlast any angst.

Reframing our minds to notice the *Wabi Sabi Love* (I highly recommend this book by Arielle Ford), a composite of two interrelated beings, pours goodness into our partners and lovingly transforms and enhances intimate relations.

From the Spanish flu to the twenty-first century's most recent pandemic, some relationships are severed in the aftermath of any disaster while others grow stronger. Many people harness their power in hopes of a better tomorrow by recommitting to a higher source of beliefs, getting in touch with their sensualness, and enlisting in an esoteric path offering humanity resilience. When we release mental and physical anguish by regulating our bodily system of acceptance – pour love and fortitude to bring us closer together rather than apart – we create elasticity that can meld a broken heart.

The collaborative echo can impress or depress our partnerships' future legacies. Reconciliation is a fundamental premise for those suffering hardship and its aftershocks, such as the pandemic. Refreshing a couple's relationship is possible, even if only one person changes their thoughts.

Acquiescing regardless of our differences allows us to aim higher. It takes courage to raise the bar by becoming a well-rounded renaissance woman.

As wise women, we possess a magnetic sensuality that ignites inventiveness to move mountains lovingly. Let us tap into this power and fearlessly conquer any challenge that comes our way. Together, we can achieve greatness and inspire others to do the same. Disconnecting from bitterness through mini-moment meditative pauses can reset our confused emotions with self-assured freedom.

As we reframe our minds from polar energies, practice mantras, listen to high-vibrational sound currents, dance from our hearts, step into nature, move in fitness and yoga studio classes, and train our bodies to uncover ourselves, we discover the secret codes of magical bliss.

When we practice gratitude like we mean it, we embody *Namaste* (I honor the light in you as it reflects the light in me). Despite opposing views, we challenge ourselves to identify with our brothers and sisters' brilliance. Observe that everyone has dealt with or is currently struggling with thoughts of unworthiness, a health crisis, and so on at some point in their lives.

Our rhythm to relay clear messages with gentler words allows us to leave each interaction with softer footprints.

Suppose any experience propels us to navigate rugged terrain by delicately rewiring circuits in our brain through a meditative state. In that case, we can rebuild, reprogram, and reframe our minds to see the other side, becoming beacons of light.

Many mind awareness tools such as conscious breath, known as life-force prana, can stimulate regions in our brain, activating the pituitary gland. Though automatic, the typical inhalation and exhalation directly influence what's going on in our mind and body – they are all interconnected. Shallow breathing shrinks our posture when our shoulders slump over the computer screen. For some, when we fall out of ease and into anxiety, our necks and back molars tighten. A dental hygienist once brought this to my attention as my wear facets were worn down. Other ongoing physical conditions and problematic muscular jaw and upper back tension often accompany this form of stress.

The Radiant Woman's Way

Breathing with intentional awareness can help you connect your power cord energies with the Universe's light.

Breath Awareness Pranayama (Life-Force Energy) Practices:

To begin, find an optimal seat on a cushioned chair with feet on the earth or place a pillow on the floor to prop your hips, with legs crossed or extended. You can also lean back on a wall. Shoulders roll back and down. Chin in alignment with the earth. Any creakiness in joints? Just observe.

Next, hone in on the breath. Is it restricted or flowing?

1. *Nadi Shodhana* (Alternate Nostril Breathing) invites us to balance the hemispheres of our brain by closing off one nostril to activate another for breath regulation. This subtle energy clearing has been practiced for centuries. It is a fundamental yoga breath awareness meditation to become alert, relaxed, and calm.

    • Eyes open or closed.

    • Place your peace fingers onto your third eye (intuition space between your eyebrows) or curl them in.

    • Using your ring finger, lightly close one nostril.

    • Inhale – hold your breath for a brief period.

    • Exhale by closing off the opposite nostril with a light dust of your thumb.

- Go back and forth, alternating with the pause in between, for 1-3 minutes.

2. *Kapalabhati,* or "Breath of Fire," is a quick-paced, detoxifying breath.[1]

   - Inhale and exhale out of your nose (or pant like a dog with tongue stretched out, inhaling and exhaling through the mouth).

   - Coordinate breath strokes with a rhythmic pumping of your stomach in and out without force.

   - Take notice of any new sensations in your body or impressions in your mind.

---

[1] Listen to your body. If pregnant, experiencing a heavy menstrual flow, or having any health conditions, practice long, deep breaths.

Chapter 7

FRIENDS, FOES, AND SISTERHOOD

"The heart has to break to get stronger."

~ Mahani

A most unfortunate encounter occurred before one of my favorite pleasures: a cooking and eating extravaganza.

Shortly after our move from a condo to a brick home in the suburbs of Bergen County, I joined our local Newcomers' Club, found common interests with other women, and quickly made friends. I was most active with the book club, playgroup, and "Afternoon Gourmet," a bi-monthly gathering that was always fun and delicious.

A few years after being an active participant and sidekick assistant in the recipe swaps and cookie exchanges, I co-chaired the gourmet food committee. Jonathan nicknamed me and my counterpart "Betty Crocker" and "Sara Lee," respectively. We would meticulously curate menus for thoughtfully planned themed events for participants to prepare and cook mouthwatering appetizers, entrees, side dishes, and desserts in advance, later to be shared at a hostess's home.

To accommodate guests for our sought-out events, we would arrive early to decorate and set up. Often, this involved rearranging furniture to make space for fold-up tables and chairs.

On a blustery mid-November day, Pat, the homeowner, greeted us at her door. Once inside, I marveled at its old-fashioned country charm – from the half-paned-glass front entrance to a low-ceilinged, wood-beamed kitchen. The open floor plan had a brick fireplace in the family room to the left. There was a small center island with a stovetop for additional food prep and the cooking demo.

Our highly anticipated Thanksgiving-themed event was sure to be a hit. Homemade mushroom risotto, along with a tasting selection of savory and sweet dishes, would be prepared with the intention that we'd make some of our favorites for our families a few weeks later for the holiday. After unloading our cars with items for the day, it was time to prep the space for guests. We placed silverware individually wrapped in cloth napkins tied with a decorative bow in the basket. Plates would soon be set out on five-foot-long tables, where women would set their steaming casserole dishes and serving platters.

We worked quickly, maneuvering Pat's couch to make room for the fold-up tables. As we slid the sofa back, we happened upon the unimaginable: a single black and white swastika[2]

---

[2] A symbol once noted for its connective connotation from Hindu mythology, early carvings, and scripture in the Western world, is now synonymous with the evil symbol of Naziism and hatred.

poker chip that had been hidden underneath the furniture. Shocked into silence, we stared with jaws hanging open at this blatant symbol of antisemitism (see blog - Glossary) and hate.

To this day, that moment remains one of the most chilling and awkward of my life. Pat immediately apologized, saying she had done her best to clean up with her family the night before because she knew I was Jewish and coming over to set up. She swiftly dusted away the evidence, adding that she was genuinely sorry I had seen it. The poker chip was from her husband's family.

I didn't know what I found more repugnant – that someone who lived in the same small town that I did, with people of all faiths, taught their kids bigotry and antisemitism, or that they did it through a game!

As I started to process what had just happened, the three of us placed pumpkin mum centerpieces atop lovely rust-orange tablecloths. Everything appeared to be in place. The ladies would soon arrive at a historical farmhouse under a picturesque snowfall, and there I was, numb from shock and betrayal. What was meant to be a day of Thanksgiving cheer became an eye-opener I never imagined.

Perversely, given what I had just seen, the event went perfectly. We relished in the ambiance and indulgence, discussing recipes during our relaxed, yet slightly formal, ladies' luncheon. Some moms had to leave early due to the forecasting of heavier snowfall. Still, many returned with their children after the early dismissal because they didn't want to miss the finale, which included coffee/tea and Viennese-style desserts.

I wore a partial facade, hiding my sadness beneath small talk and smiles. There I was, living in a town and a world that still harbored evil and, worse yet, taught the next generations to do the same.

Later that evening, I retold the poker chips story to Jonathan. The homeowner said it had been "their family inheritance." I was disgusted by Pat's repulsive heirloom. Knowing we'd be together again with having children of similar age and other newcomers' events made things worse. I recall a feeling of helplessness, even after Jonathan and I contacted our rabbi, and shared this disheartening encounter with a few close friends. I rehashed it with my "gourmet" counterpart, who was also stunned by the revelation – I was a victim of circumstance. Nothing erased my pain; I felt I had a new understanding of what others have dealt with due to their skin color, social and ethnic class, and race since the beginning of time.

Today, I recognize that this incident was meant to be remembered. Nobody deserves to be judged based on religious values or upbringing. Narrow perspectives and age-old myths must change so history does not repeat itself. Although Pat's reaction disturbed me, I chose to get along and was in her company on other occasions, shining and smiling with pride and purpose. Despite wanting to restart the conversation, I knew I had to put aside her family's ignorance. Eventually, to my relief, her family moved to New England.

Living with purpose, where we might never change anyone's mind but continue to operate from a place of love and kindness, always wins. Until we feel it ourselves, we might not understand antisemitism or other forms of ignorance. The sun shines on everyone. It does not discriminate. Love abolishes evil. Injustice motivates people to advocate for equal rights.

While in college, my friend from Rhode Island became curious about my heritage. I'd soon be heading back to New Jersey for the extended holiday break. "Why don't you have a Christmas tree?" she asked. "Because I'm Jewish," I replied.

Years later, our lives intersected again as neighbors. I enjoyed her home's welcoming atmosphere and festive décor, and our annual meetups at Rockefeller Center's dazzling tree and Saks Fifth Avenue's light show—followed by gourmet meals, a traditional Secret Santa gift exchange, and chocolate-covered strawberries and graham crackers—became cherished highlights.

One moment, however, left us in hysterics. We laughed when we learned that her youngest daughter had raised her hand and said "yes" in class when the teacher asked who celebrated Hanukkah. The innocence of a child's experience, after sharing our family's rituals of eating gelt (chocolate coins), spinning dreidels, and lighting the menorah on one of the eight nights, gave her and others invited to our home a glimpse into a festive holiday less familiar to them, yet rich with the warmth of its oil-burning lights.

Celebrating with people who are different from us allows us to see the world through their eyes. Over the years, each family's milestones, from Communions to Bar and Bat Mitzvahs, has deepened our friendship and underscored the profound impact of appreciating one another for who we are.

Relationships, like everything else, are here for a reason. Over time, they might ripen with age and move in a new direction for better or worse, in sickness and health. Recall that friend, mentioned earlier, who made up little stories about other people when I was with her, which let me know she could just as easily do the same to me.

Although tempted, I never joined a sorority, backing away when many of my peers visited various houses during the second semester of my freshman year. I wanted no part in the comparison game: "My sorority is better than yours." I chose to be an outside observer instead of joining one tribe over another, yet, sometimes, I felt left out when friends got ready for their social mixers, formal dances, and secret meetings.

Oh, how eager they were to join and obey laws and ethical codes of sisterhood while bonding together in a way I didn't know much about. I didn't want to put my fate in someone else's hands who decided to enlist or reject me. For many, this was a gateway to a community that would evolve into leadership roles and life-long friendships. For me, there was too much unknown pressure and not enough of a nice vibe to ignore it. At the time, I didn't realize I was staying true to myself by refusing to be graded, dissected, dissed, or dismissed. I also refused to exclude anyone based on the color of their skin or religion – checklists and gossip derived by bias added division – and I certainly wasn't willing to do it for the coveted party perks sisterhood offered.

My decision benefited me in several ways. As mentioned, I sold my beaded jewelry collection in sorority houses – an experience that elevated and suited me. If I had chosen one sorority, I would not have had the invitation to visit others. Besides, I preferred building relationships independent of others' opinions.

Years later, as a mom and supporter of a local organization, I attended, placed an ad in their journal, and was enthusiastic about supporting the cause. However, upon entering the main ballroom alone, I felt excluded even after meeting up with a group of women I knew. Nonetheless, I was all dressed up and felt grateful for the opportunity to be present. When seated for dinner, a woman I knew turned her head away from me the entire evening! *No sweat off my back;* I prefer talking to strangers, sitting in silence, or leaving the room before dessert for a change of view rather than pretending to be someone I'm not.

It is crucial to distinguish between tactics that create division and the understanding that it is not about us or our egos. As deflated as I felt from the woman's cold shoulder, I extended an invisible offer of heartfelt compassion. Had I imagined the scene of being shunned by another or was it an innocent gesture? And then I realized it was important to take myself out of the equation and shift my attention to what mattered most: the gala's cause benefiting families of children enduring treatment for brain cancer. When focused on helping another, many tensions dissolve. We don't always know why someone isn't meshing in our sphere.

One thing I have come to better understand in trying to uncover myself is that "hurt people hurt people." Although we might seem happy, internal struggles or idle gossip can jeopardize benevolence. However, as Radiant Women, we can disrupt adverse effects by disengaging from energies that don't belong to us.

Relationships Transformed as a Test of Time

One day in late spring, I received group text messages about a potential getaway with friends.

Should I stay or venture out? It would be the first time leaving my daughter overnight since she'd undergone a recent surgery.

As destination suggestions and dates were proposed, I sensed some aspects of the trip wouldn't run smoothly – an intuitive inkling soon proved accurate.

When we first gathered, I felt a warm embrace of friendship. Yet in a flash, the mood changed. By late afternoon of our first day, we arranged to leave early for dinner by boat. I asked two friends what they were wearing – my concern about covering up my skin when the sun's rays were still intense presented me with an extra layer of heated tension. Upon one friend's comment proposing we change our next night's dinner plans, I hoped we would still hit the proposed "hot spot."

After my simple question and comment before our outing, another long-time friend snapped, "I don't like your voice. You always mess things up."

Bewildered and stunned, I did my best to set this scuffle aside for our time together. Before departing, though, I attempted to revisit our unsettled confrontation. Her response: I was "passive-aggressive." My jaw dropped. Another nearby friend patted me on the shoulder, and I shuddered that instant, knowing those words had been uttered behind my back before.

In my mind, I reenacted past encounter scenes.

What had I done to irritate her that I was unaware of? Were my texts in the group thread, sent before securing our destination, unclear? Who was I to disagree with her opinion? What was I meant to unravel in myself so I could be a better person?

The New Oxford Dictionary defines passive-aggressive as "characterized by indirect resistance to the demands of others and avoidance of confrontation."

Even though her verbal lashing and disregard for my feelings caught me off-guard, I knew it was not up to me to change her mind.

I contemplated, wanting to clear the air, knowing our friendship history would bring us together again. Once home, I left a few messages to see if we could meet in person, with no response. I then decided not to go down the alley again. There was no room for immediate change. Although our relationship felt off balance and her hurtful remarks lingered, they were not meant to be revisited then. Our friendship shifted. I no longer call if I am having a difficult day; however, I respect her opinion, and we have remained good friends. We cannot make everyone see our point of view. Although her words once felt sharp, time softened their edge. I chose to show up, knowing that true friendship allows space for mending relations.

We might never understand their opinions or actions, yet we can accept our differences by looking through the lens of love.

On another occasion, I overheard the same friend gossiping about another woman. She referred to her as "passive-aggressive." I smiled to myself.

Oh my, that's her go-to diagnosis for someone she disagrees with or miscommunicates their emotions.

I have also heard the term used by other friends and relatives. Were women of society avoiding their emotions? Was it from depressive states gone unnoticed or unresolved? We might deter misconceived finger-pointers if we healed our wounds, refrained from speaking until we clarified what we meant, and stated our most authentic feelings.

By questioning someone who might not fully express themselves, we move toward compassion instead of harassing, blaming, and shaming.

Trisha Mayduria, the Sanskrit name I received upon graduating from my first yoga training, means "thirsting sweet nectar." My teachers saw this in me: a desire to evolve and share positivity and calm with others, including a thirst to learn and enhance my relationships with spiritual/deeper connections.

In Gurmukhi, from the Kundalini lineage, I received the name *"Puranjeet."* Living up to its meaning prompted me to discover my life's *purna* (perfection) aspects. When we assemble in nature's temples, connect with humanity by reaching for *"jai,"* which is a Hindi word derived from Sanskrit, meaning victoriousness, we roar with a lioness' instinct for survival.

We align with patience by wholeheartedly accepting another being for their unique personality (instead of hoping they change to satisfy our desires). When we resist thick woods of jealousy and resentment by no longer drinking venomous repetition about what we don't like in someone, we instead choose love. When we begin to lean on one common ground, our human heartbeats, we can connect on an even plane. Hey, the annoying telemarketer who disturbed your dinner in this lifetime (or, if you believe, in a past one) might have been your relative if circumstances were different.

The Radiant Woman's Way

Implement a Friendliness Practice to develop compassion, love, and kindness for yourself and others. Encourage double rainbows and simple joys to appear.

Prep

By easing your or someone else's pain – and celebrating your and or their accomplishments – you can embrace the Radiant Woman within.

Metta (Friendliness) Meditation

- Become aware of yourself by focusing on a feeling of joy or pain for yourself or someone to whom you want to bring peace, calm, and tranquility.

- Beam love from your heart while imagining golden light flooding your body.

- Repeat to yourself, "May I be happy, well, and free."

- Bring a dear friend to mind as vividly as possible and think of their admirable qualities.

- Feel your friendship bond by noticing the potential blossoming.

- Think and repeat to yourself, "May you be happy, well, and free."

- Next, bring someone you barely know (i.e., you have passed by them before, perhaps made small talk, and would welcome a longer conversation with them one day) into your mind.

- Think and repeat to yourself, "May you be happy, well, and free."

- For the final part, bring a difficult relationship to your mind and (as hard as this might sound) send out good thoughts and well wishes.

- Think and repeat to yourself, "May you be happy, well, and free."

The key to building a healthier reaction/relationship with someone you perceive as different or difficult to get along with is to list anything you have in common (i.e., breath and DNA[3] in a broad sense). Did you know all humans are 99.9 percent identical in their genetic makeup? Our differences lie in the 0.1 percent. Noticing basic similarities in someone can help us clear the air and shed new light on our relationships.

---

[3] Pflanzer, Lydia Ramsey and Lee, Samantha. "Our DNA is 99.9% the Same as the Person Next to Us – and We're Surprisingly Similar to A Lot of Other Living Things. April 3, 2018. Business Insider. https://www.businessinsider.com/comparing-genetic-similarity-between-humans-and-other-things-2016-5

Chapter 8

EAST MEETS WEST: NAVIGATING PERSONAL HEALTH

If you believe it will work out, you will see opportunities.
If you believe it won't, you will see obstacles.

~ Wayne Dyer

One night in January 2012, as I was getting ready for bed, a peculiar, chaotic sensation entered my body with explosive commotion. It was beyond my control and wildest imagination. Felt like a ton of bricks landed on my upper back while something extraterrestrial pounced on my shoulders. There were also strange pumping sensations in my veins.

Subsequent incidents involved an internal "punching" feeling that left my body drained and challenged me at the core. Medical mysteries caused me to speculate with alarm. Annalisa Pastore, my integrative physician of Chi Medicine (see Appendix), ordered lab tests that revealed low white blood cell count and high histamine and inflammation markers.

> "My goal is to educate and empower patients
> so that they may tune into their own needs and
> guidance. Overreliance on anyone outside of
> oneself to hold the answers for one's healing or
> to be a container for one's fears and anxieties
> ultimately stunts one's growth. The guide should
> illuminate the path but allow each person to
> journey in their way." ~*Annalisa Pastore*

By then, I was already on the path to naturally healing my body and calming the never-ending, swirling thoughts in my mind.

Jin Shin Jyutsu® (JSJ), a Japanese healing modality, became integral to my routine. My friend Audrey, now a health and wellness coach, introduced me to it the year our sons met in kindergarten. Pregnant with my fourth, I would feel exhausted upon arriving for a session. However, after leaving, I felt rejuvenated and optimistic. It harmonized my body.

JSJ focuses on utilizing the healing powers of our hands. We hold our thumbs or fingers in specific positions to release tension.

For example, if we have a stomachache or observed worry in our minds, we can hold one of our thumbs. Within seconds to minutes, the mental or physical ache might disappear. If we are frustrated, we can try holding our index finger. Within seconds to minutes, we might feel our body's muscle tension relax at ease.

Acupuncture uses light needling to communicate with our meridians (invisible Chinese acupressure points). A skilled practitioner can help release blocked pathways deep beneath the skin or work with the body's gross anatomy (a medical term for its prevalent notable systems) when the treatment to restore function is surface-deep.

While experiencing unusual symptoms, I taught and participated in yoga and meditation classes in various studio spaces, supporting others' personal growth. Although I kept my tingling hands/feet and body aches private, I found support in these communities.

Where had this heightened inflammation begun?

At age 13, I visited a dermatologist hoping for a topical cream to treat a nickel-sized spot on my back.

But that was NOT the case for me then or in my future.

I will never forget the day the doctor uttered these words to me...

"Marla, you have a disease."

I was stunned!

I was just a teen trying to fit in!

But you know how they say your most significant challenges are your biggest blessings?

I am living proof.

That shocking and confusing time in my adolescence led me to be here with you.

What is life if you are not fulfilling your purpose or making your impact on those around you?

It ended up that I was diagnosed with vitiligo, a skin disorder that causes loss of pigmentation. (The same condition caused Michael Jackson to lose his skin color.)

The doctor asked if I was experiencing any stress that could have triggered the onset. Hmmm, teenage hormones, the recent start of my menstrual cycle? "No," I replied when he asked if the family had suffered a loss or anything that might have jolted my system. He went on to tell me that while not life-threatening, vitiligo is life-altering and, in most cases, leads to thyroid problems.

As doctors predicted, it went beyond my skin's surface level. Decades later, after a thorough exam by an endocrinologist whereby he asked me to tip my neck back and swallow as he felt the exposed gland, he diagnosed me with Hashimoto's. I went on medication to adjust this gland known for regulating hormones and to this day, like millions of women around the world, have found hair and weight loss challenging to regulate.

As for my two-toned complexion, it became prominent in summer due to more exposed skin and the sun naturally tanning me even with sunscreen. Sitting out in the sun with a psoralen's treatment, I tried to regain my pigment. It would freckle in the white spaces, and then I'd lose the pigment again. Bleaching is an alternative recommendation; however, I never chose that route, always holding out hope for a cure.

Strangers sometimes questioned if I had suffered burns when they saw my irregularly patterned skin. One day, while lounging near a lake in my bathing suit, a young girl got scared and asked if I was contagious. I shrank. The girl appeared content after her mother reassured her that she was safe sitting beside me. However, I couldn't help but wonder if I was okay.

Could I live contentedly if it were not in my control? Over the years the loss of pigmentation had spread across my body like a slow-burning but uncontrolled fire. As I prayed for my immune system to cool down and stop its constant alterations in discoloration, the cosmetic display altered my self-perception.

For centuries and even today, individuals have been unfairly treated, discriminated against, and disregarded because of their differences. By prioritizing empathy, we can generate more thoughtful responses to our queries.

What could we do to prevent or stop inflammation from spreading its fury?

If *dis-ease* meant the body wanted to heal from being out of ease, then it was up to everyone, case by case, to invigorate and challenge their bodies when they feel depleted. Negative thoughts influence our minds, weaken our immune system's recovery, and settle in our cells. According to evolution, humans have become fearful nine out of ten times to keep us safe. It's no wonder there is a pandemic of people experiencing inflammation. "I'm so tired" is an all-too-familiar symptom after a restless night.

As I aged and after having children, many hormonal imbalances arose, including premature hot flashes in my early forties.

On a few girls' nights out, I enjoyed a delicious meal containing many spices and food groups accompanied by two glasses of wine, only to end up with mysterious rashes – histamine reactions. One evening, I felt my airways restricted to the point where the ladies I was out with debated taking me to the ER. After a reliable source advised Benadryl, it gave me quick-acting relief. The bigger question remained: What was I allergic to?

Alarmed, I thought to myself, *One ailment at a time.* Strange muscle cramps with extremity tingles, brain fog where I said the wrong word when another was intended, blurred vision, and perplexing "thumps" in my eyes became bothersome. While practicing yoga to release stress, I found myself shifting further into my role of caring for myself.

Dr. Pastore ordered MRI imaging of my brain. Thankfully, the detections of lesions related to multiple sclerosis and other conditions were ruled out. Yet, what was causing my mysterious stomach rashes, constant fatigue, inflamed joints, and extremity sensations?

Throughout my health scare, I meditated and prayed; I confided with my yoga mentor, Sheryl, about my fears. She listened without judgment. Self-study enabled me to reshape my words.

March 24, 2015

Sweet Sheryl (SS),

> *My radiating nerve issue, allergic reaction that feels like my esophagus and throat are burning and closing in, and all my recent health issues have me feeling low like I am dying. I even talked to Jonathan about our wills. I want to be my best self and feel better. I use my voice in yoga*

training workshop settings and in my everyday communi-
cations, only when it's my turn to speak.

With blood at its core, I know I have a will to live. I must
battle and tend to my medical woes now since physical
health is mental health. Perhaps my throat-closing issue is
trying to tell me something regarding listening and trusting
my intuition too?

Mostly, I don't want to complain. I'm full of gratitude.

Love, Marla

March 25, 2015

Reply from SS,

"Oh, sweet one. Your pain is my pain. I wish every day
for your physical pain to subside."

Symptoms persisted. A neurologist ordered a test for me to
check if I had residual nerve damage. The intense procedure
revealed I did not. Years later, upon further investigation, I
learned that my form of neuropathy differed from those with
diabetes. Like many who might be inflamed in their wrist,
knee, hip, and other joints or have other inflamed conditions,
I was experiencing the aftereffects of toxic overload. The
inflammation sought an escape. And, by not being released, it
manifested as tingles in my extremities.

I was intuitively guided to attend "Conscious Communications," a Level 2 Kundalini (yoga of awareness) teacher training in New York City led by world-renowned yoga teacher

Gurmukh Khalsa. Each morning began with a 4 a.m. *sadhana* (early before sunrise) meditation. On day two, I was partnered with a woman who shared that she was an integrative doctor. As we supported each other in our breathing awareness techniques and new material we'd learned, I shared some of my recent unexplained medical symptoms and lab work results with her. She listened attentively and recommended that I ask my current doctor to order some less routine blood tests to see if I had active Lyme disease or any long-term consequences from co-infections. Out-of-pocket expenses would more than likely occur.

As she questioned me, I remembered being bitten by a tick in my twenties. Could it be that the bacterial aftereffect remained in my body so many years after the venom was deposited? Indeed, it felt like something was trapped inside me, wreaking havoc on my immune system.

The whole time, as I was experiencing neurological deficits, horrid headaches, and unresponsive reflexes when my doctors banged under my knee, I was also teaching yoga classes for adults and children. I developed my branding and created flyers for after-school wellness programs, volunteered for an organization, *Kula for Karma*, bringing mindfulness to populations that generally would not have had access to yoga and other holistic health and wellness instruction. It felt good to serve others and forget about my woes.

For a few years before, during, and after my health scare, I met with two women for standing, semi-private yoga Zen stretch sessions. Gillian's bright blue eyes twinkled as she rolled in on her scooter. Nancy, though petite and slightly frail, was strong in spirit and brought honest warmth. She used a cane in one hand and held the wall with her other as she shuffled her feet. She was a bit younger than my mom and had younger grand-children. Though MS was a debilitating disease, they both had so much pride as they headed down *Naturally Yoga's* hall. If I helped to roll Gillian over so Sheryl could stretch her under-side, I took care to be gentle with her limbs. With Nancy, whom I mainly assisted, I held her feet, wiggled her toes back and forth, placed the heel of my hands into the arches of her feet, bent and straightened her legs, rubbed her arms, rolled her wrists, and massaged her temples for a whole-body experience. At first, I followed Sheryl's lead. However, I ultimately relied on my intuition and incorporated tai yoga stretch modalities that I had learned early on in my first yoga teacher training.

We bonded over calming chimes and ethereal sounds in an environment that promoted holistic therapeutic benefits. I continued to greet and care for Nancy and Gillain, never let-ting either know when pain and muscle spasms enveloped me.

And then, as my involuntary eye twitches became more fre-quent, those specialized tests revealed that my neurological effects were indeed the result of long-time Lyme disease.

Odd protocols started. A Lyme specialist prescribed doxycycline. Though I had an allergic rash reaction and my mouth tasted metal, I persevered from one harsh antibacterial prescription to another. Along with medicine, I placed twenty tincture dropper drops under my tongue, twenty minutes away from food, twice a day for a year. Held it in my mouth and counted for a minute before I swallowed. The bitter herb medicinal tincture supple-ments, preserved in alcohol solutions, fought off two detected co-infections for Lyme. One was *Babesia*, the other *Bartonella*.

The residue from shedding toxins made me feel worse. For months, strange regimens sank me lower due to the Herxheimer, or "Herx," response – a natural process triggered by a greater prevalence of endotoxins. This attempt to expel dead bacteria from the body takes time. The buildup of toxic waste can leave the patient feeling lethargic, with chronic inflammation and poor memory and concentration. This is when the nervous system flairs worsen before it feels better. Extraneous substances are released when harmful microorganisms and bacteria are destroyed or die off. As bacteria in my body were damaged, endotoxins penetrated my bloodstream.

While having an inner core group to support us is critical, the most crucial healing aspect is detaching from our body and mind and sensing our human spirit vibrating in good health.

Decline an invitation if you feel too scheduled, unwind with a mini-moment, pause to give yourself extra strength and vitality. If you fall, do what is in your wheelhouse to pick yourself up, and go forward by shifting your mood to access your radiant shine.

I'm confident that my alternative solution practices better prepared me for life's snafus and gave me the courage to persist when the neurologist told me there were no other options. My gut instincts guided me to seek further avenues.

One day, it felt like fragments of leaves or random dust had blown into my eyes. An eye exam revealed this as another autoimmune response known as iritis. This caused me alarm – if I didn't tend to the iritis properly it could worsen and cause blindness.

The protocol treatments required a heavy steroid ointment two times a day with eye drops four times a day. The regimen was tapered off over six weeks with follow-up eye exams in between until my inflammation normalized. Organic rose washes and sprays have become my preferred natural supplements to support my eye health, unless otherwise specified.

On another visit to the ophthalmologist, the doc peered, prodded, pulled my eyelids down, and asked me to close my eyes on a piece of paper. In a snap, a prescription for dry eyes, a medication I'd need for life, was written. I had no symptoms. *Maybe it was the result of my previous rounds of steroid treatments,* I thought to myself. I never filled that script.

Most doctors, though highly skilled and specialized, are trained to treat patients once they become injured or ill. As a majority, medical professionals and nurses care, but some don't have the extra five minutes to answer their patients' additional questions and concerns. Theories, research, and developed treatments have been scientifically proven to work for some and not for others.

Customizing an individual's strategy based on their specific ailment and ever-changing symptoms in relation to the cellular mechanics of their body is for research scientists to investigate and prove before a doctor suggests it. In this fuzzy territory, we the patients are left to advocate for ourselves. Due to increased quotas in a demanding industry, the time with our medical doctors has shortened.

Prioritizing tailored care by complementing mainstream medicine with alternative options such as apothecary and supplemental herbs like arnica for bruising and compounded turmeric (curcumin), which fights inflammation and acts as an antioxidant.

I'm grateful to the medical industry for its scientific discoveries to uncover rare disorders and technological precision, including robotic and laser-based innovations, and biological advancements extending our loved ones' lives. Yet, getting to the root cause of disease and inflammation is often unclear. The lack of educated guesses can exacerbate a patient's stress. Adding complementary refinement to our prescriptive health and wellness is paramount to radiance.

Stress impacts our health. Nature walks, guided and personal home practice meditations, sound baths with brass gongs, charged crystals (from the sun, moon, and earth energy), and brass bowls offer healing vibrations to improve our overall mood and health. As a result of being deeply relaxed, we become less reactive and more neutral when faced with diverging opinions.

Forest bathing was termed a Japanese practice in the 1980s. The physiological and psychological exercise called *shinrin-yoku* ("taking in the forest atmosphere") was twofold: offering an "eco-antidote to tech-boom burnout and to inspire residents to reconnect with the country's forests."[4]

Many other scientific studies of trees have proven that the oxygen we get from trees heals our cells, just like we offer carbon dioxide to the forests.

---

[4] Fitzgerald, Sunny. October 18, 2019. "The Secret to Mindful Travel? A Walk in the Woods." National Geographic. https://www.nationalgeographic.com/travel/article/forest-bathing-nature-walk-health#:~:text=In%20the%201990s%2C%20researchers%20began,the%20practice%20is%20not%20new.

Answers come from our readiness to examine our internal thoughts while excavating to heal from inside out and outside in; allowing outdoor surroundings and our interactions, be it with nature and people; and integrating Eastern and Western tips on treating medical ailments.

And to think that when I saw the neurologist before I had a diagnosis, he barely acknowledged my neuropathy, strange feelings, and achy joints. He just stared at me when I asked if it could be due to Lyme. This tick-borne disease doesn't get proper funds or attention because there is neither a cure nor conclusive lab work, whether you were bitten one day, week or ten years ago. More studies are needed. There is current talk of the canine vaccine becoming available for humans, which might help long-time Lyme patients gain respectful attention, as those with long Covid have.

As we better understand our role in stress, we can sustain life through health and wellness modalities geared towards longevity. We can protect our electromagnetic field by cultivating an awareness of how to use protective shields, as naturally as we adjust to changing temperatures – layering or removing rain gear, winter coats, spring jackets, or capes, one step at a time. By peeling back the armor of our facade, we can uncover the truth of our soul's calling. This process involves implementing awareness tools and taking responsibility for our actions, rather than placing blame on others. We can alter our health from "labeled diseases," often noted for insurance purposes. As far-fetched as it may sound, healing from illness or, at best, prolonging our lives with a will to survive is possible. When we free ourselves from a referenced medical condition(s), we detach from their limited diagnoses and, in some cases, experience unexplained improvements or recoveries. This concept allows us to explore the interconnections of the mind-body-spirit instead of remaining stuck with a label.

My initial travels abroad expanded my independent perspective. It gave me a lifetime of memorable reflections. Decades later, when I altered my mind and body perception, I intermingled with people from different neighborhoods again. I also met other holistic practitioners as I trained for intuitive wellness certifications. Many gathered in person and – during the pandemic – online, embracing personal growth with students of life from countries around the world. I have had dozens of in-depth, intense, honest discussions with women in Zoom rooms. Social interactions elevate our spirit. The physical distance does not matter if the heart and soul are present.

During a Reiki session, a practitioner uses attuned energy to bring tender neutrality to their client. This traditional Japanese modality allows our bodies to rest, relax, and rejuvenate.

When a healer places their hand in positions that hover over or are placed lightly on the body, traveling through energetic fields, the result is a sense of silence.

Having someone to sit with your energy in person or for a long-distance session can positively affect your nervous system and lead to lasting benefits.

It is helpful if a client remains receptive during the healing session.

Reiki encourages the body to respond beyond surface-level stimuli and reach the underlying organs. Through this process, an invisible transmission commutes through a driving agent to rejuvenate one's life force energy.

The silent space and sense of care one can
feel during a session offer resolution to clear
out the inside voice.

Even if the allotted time slot contracted is remote, this synergistic measure can reduce tension. The practitioner temporarily excuses herself from the equation. She intuitively adjusts her specifics to the individual's body. Their quickened heartbeat subsides, and their breath becomes elongated. If an outside voice comes (i.e., "What am I cooking for dinner?"), she returns to the conductive energy. She trusts her client's natural wisdom's ability to transform heated emotions – extinguishing depressed thoughts and removing barriers so energy can flow freely.

I can vouch for myself as a Reiki master and receiver. On many occasions, I have either cried or gained a fresher outlook on issues I wanted to control yet had to let go of. I, too, have witnessed the transformation in others. Its benefits might not be noticeable to the naked eye, but this kind of work is well worth the effort and money to schedule.

When we introduce any new substance into our body, medically, scientifically, or metaphysically proven, we must trust its interactive properties where matter is composed; the informant determines the process. What we put into our bodies – conscious breath, thoughts, and food – adds charge to our existence. We are the ones who can reshape our destiny.

The pituitary gland (introduced in Chapter 5) is a pea-sized structure at the base of the brain that releases what's sometimes referenced as the "cuddle" or "love" hormone. It appreciates heart-centered attention.

When a *Reiki* master offers infinite measures of steadfast compassion, the client benefits from an environment that facilitates the transfer of positive energy to their body. Again, it helps if the client trusts the process. Elongated breathing patterns reduce stress and keep our master gland healthy. With the courage to take an alternative route, our life-force energy expands. So many diseases and disorders are triggered by stress. It's no wonder that Reiki programs are increasingly being offered in hospitals and wellness centers, as studies have shown it aids in restoring equilibrium and speedier patient recovery.

I found peace when attending health and wellness retreats, yoga and meditation classes. In nature's awestruck glory, I saw my imperfect perfection. The notion that "ignorance is bliss" never gives us a free pass. Once we know, we know. Our responsibility is to adapt to what we know by shifting our tempered minds. We cannot undo the pre-digital era but return to inner harmony by synthesizing our natural rhythms.

Energetic Body

Though invisible to the naked eye or a surgical lens, the movement of our cosmic energy systems exists for anyone to discover, observe, and be in a relationship with. If we pay attention to healing these vortexes from within, we can use them as an explorative map for intuitive measures. The communication between breath, body, and mind influences our subtle systems consisting of focal points, often called chakra centers. These overlapping channels, connected by breath, are influenced by meditations.

Where did the conversation of chakras (literally "wheels") originate? According to Medical News Today, "The earliest written record of chakras comes from the Vedas, which are ancient Indian texts that describe the philosophy of yoga." These conceptual signs have served as jump-off entry points that have influenced our body's energy for thousands of years. The spinning chakras (wheels) overlap – from the root of our seats to the solar plexus power, heart center, throat, intuition, into ethers of angelic realms. The colorful wheels correspond to these portals in our body, each an opportunity to become rooted in love and acceptance and rise above the murky waters into our higher self.

Similar colors identified by deep meditators in different Asian regions thousands of years ago after practicing were documented.

These wheels of overlapping colors range from:

First chakra – clay earth – base of the spine is primal, grounded and supported.

Second chakra – sacral orange – below your belly button, a sensual creativity.

Third chakra – solar lemon – in your navel center, core-powered solar plexus strength.

Fourth chakra – heart green or fuchsia. It is noted for its unstruck sound since most sounds result from friction. Polarity. In flux with space around us inducing the cosmic sound of *OM*.

Fifth chakra – blue ocean – is located in your throat, the voice of reason.

Sixth chakra – indigo to violet – third-eye space between eyebrows, igniting intuition.

Seventh chakra – top of the head, iridescent, incandescent, and translucent; it encapsulates an aurora borealis rainbow.

Abundant joy can be juiced into our daily routines through the rainbow chakra centers, which offer hope for a new perspective on improving our relationship with ourselves. Noticing how we influence our body and mind trickles into everything we do.

The nurturer nurtures herself with enough energy to encourage the young and the old. From aging in-laws, parents, mentors, students, peers, children, and pets, the purpose of knowledge is to take what we know and use it for a caring purpose.

When we treat our bodies as sacred temples, we honor the mightiest holy site – the temple space in our hearts.

Just as wounded skin regenerates after injury, our inner resilience adjusts. With ardent wonder, we can rise to the occasion, flex our bodies by elongating the spine, and etch our minds through mini-moment pauses, embracing life's illustrious splendor.

Getting out of the reptilian brain (which reacts to fear with instinctual primal behavior that controls our motives), into the limbic brain (which processes emotional responses) allows us to live more from the heart. We become truly "hue-man" (a colorful hue manifested), enjoying life as it is now, allowing physical embodiment to blossom.

Creating new habits, like meditation or other conscious living practices, reshapes our desires for divinity.

The Radiant Woman searches for clues and answers. She listens to her intuitive mind, defers from temporary Band-Aid medications that might only cover up the core hindrance. When a diagnostic obstacle arises, she researches and considers changes as a formula to eradicate or improve the management of any health crises for herself and her loved ones. She aims to raise her spirit and live her best life each day.

The human condition contributes to environmental factors and internal cellular wells that govern who we become through regenerated cells. Where we live and who we surround ourselves with change throughout the trajectory of our lives. Fine-tuning adjustments allow us to add critical insight into what works and what doesn't regarding health and wellness care options. Yes, much is predetermined; progress requires a desire to shift the nature of our humanness. Turning our footpath into a walking meditation, placing each foot gently on the ground – thinking peace with one and thinking love with the other – promotes conscious actions to carry over in our relationship connections.

Gathering with like-minded women in online and in-person communities can help us move through stuck energies and heal. When meeting in prayer groups with high-vibration settings for someone we love whose body is in crisis, we can move energy to guide another through their plight.

Complementing Western medical procedures with alternative therapies like acupuncture and lymphatic drainage massage can replace or speed up recovery by steering the mind and body into alignment with health and wellness.

I often dry brush to shed skin and activate pores before a shower. It also rejuvenates when I feel sleepy before going out or want to work on a project. I also use **Abhyanga,** an ayurvedic oil massage that can be applied before bed, upon rising, or any time of day.

Use a soothing high-grade essential oil with an emulsifier like coconut oil; apply it under your armpits, soles of feet, in your belly button. This ritual, used daily or occasionally, reduces inflammation and regenerates your body and skin with a youthful, healthy and happy glow.

What to Expect in a Traditional Yoga Class?

If you're interested in yoga for its physical endurance and mental health benefits, a great starting point would be to attend an intro or basic yoga class online or in person. I enjoy all yoga levels, as they allow me to engage muscles and refine the poses. When practicing, it's recommended to wear comfortable, athleisure clothing.

In addition, incorporating Ujjayi's "Ocean breath" technique can help to further calm your system by promoting better circulation. This technique involves gently closing your lips, breathing in and out slowly through your nose, and creating a guttural Darth Vader-like sound in your throat. It's a great technique to use throughout your day, as it can be done quietly and without drawing attention to yourself.

Sun salutations (known as *Surya namaskar)* welcome the morning sun and stimulate our circulatory system. One of its primary functions is to protect our bodies against disease and infections. This series of positions, which flow from Downward and Upward Facing Dogs into a plank with lunges and one knee on the floor as arms stretched high, brings fresh nutrients to the pituitary tissue.

A Sun Salutation Series A or B salutation can be practiced any time of day. That said, when we greet the sun upon its rising and use tools during sunset, our body receives extra warmed-up benefits.

Inversions such as Legs Up the Wall (lower back on the floor, one hip near the wall, and swing both legs up for a vital posture) or headstands (for which you can use blocks under shoulders and a wall to assist you) reverse your blood flow – also known to benefit the pituitary gland and its functions. Poses that involve bending forward, like Seated Wide Leg Forward Bend, are soothing for the nerves.

Practicing energy awareness tools through "The 5 M's of Meditation" – music, movement, mantra, mudra, and magic – are practical trailblazers that deepen our consciousness.

The Radiant Woman's Way

To consciously invite the sunlight with gratitude for its rise, try this mini **Radiance Sun Salute** to amplify your glow.

- Stand or remain seated.
- Close eyes with hands on heart.
- Think of the grateful grace of the sun.

- Reach your arms up to the sky.
- Arch back to welcome in the light.
- Lengthen your spine with arms still up.
- Let your elbows bend so the middle fingers lightly touch at the top.
- Still touching at the middle fingers, bring an invisible circular ball of light down, passing through your heart.
- Lower releasing hands to sides.
- In a sweeping motion, reach arms up again.
- Repeat a few times.
- Next, reach arms high with feet hip-width apart.
- Reach your arms up to the sky.
- Hinge forward with knees slightly bent to any degree toward the floor. [5]
- Touch anywhere on your legs, the ground (or blocks).
- Float arms back up to the sky.
- Bow forward and keep going at your own pace.
- You can stay in any one area for thirty seconds.
- Practice for 3-5 minutes.

---

[5] If you experience back discomfort, visualize the hinging. Remain standing in a mountain pose (feet on earth with palms down to sides facing open). Reach arms to the sky, and bring them back down to sides.

Chapter 9

AGENT GRACE: THE EBB AND FLOW OF TIMELESS AGING

*"You can't use up creativity. The more you use,
the more you have."*

~ Maya Angelou

From the moment we let out our first cry to the moment we die, we are open vessels to learn something new. We come into this world sponges, ready to be saturated and squeezed. Born to discover, take risks, and thrive. As children, we're tested through trial and error, developing reflexes so we don't get burned.

We are challenged to repair broken relationships at every phase, just like when our computer glitches. By strengthening our auric awareness, we redirect our psyche to navigate roadblocks as a prerequisite to disrupting conditioned behaviors meant to change. And let's not forget to have fun, as the word *lila* in Sanskrit suggests. It means pastime or drama and being playful.

As a young girl, my "not good enough" complex erupted in dance classes to required math, history, and gym classes. Fluctuating hormones and menstrual cramps were accompanied by bodily discomfort and embarrassment. As a developing teen, whenever I looked in the mirror and saw my one-hundred-pound (on a good day), five-foot-one frame, I compared myself negatively to the taller, slimmer girls. A brunette, I longed to be blonde. I felt cursed by the curves, breasts, and hips God had given me. I didn't realize I was giving my power away by not loving myself initially. I led a dual life – one of opportunity, where the whole world was in my hands, and another in which I constantly diminished my shine.

When beer and grain alcohol flowed out of the nozzle, my inhibitions, personality, and spirit lifted, hoping to be noticed by the one-star soccer player, a group of rowdy frat boys, and the star quarterback. By my senior year of college, my friends and I had developed an affinity for White Russians (Kahlua, vodka, and cream) and Cosmopolitans. I refined my taste for red, white, and rosé. On occasion, I stumbled, fell, and lost balance and control.

During my busiest days as a young mom with active kids, an endless cycle of carpools and undertakings left me yearning for peace. I felt my spirit unravel. Pouring a glass or two of red wine midweek occasionally when not in a social setting helped me unwind and forget about tomorrow's worries. However, I didn't want to follow a route that could lead to an addictive (See Appendix) behavior such as a coping mechanism.

It is a conscious choice to fill our bodies with toxins, just as it is a choice to enter an ambitious and ardent path to break a habit. That was what I did each time I communed at yoga. I resisted the temptation to numb my feelings. Meditation, such as focusing on a candle and repeating mantras like "I am bountiful, blissful, and beautiful" for three to five minutes, has expanded my quality of life with increased perception. Seeking help from trained professionals and programs is also an option. Touching a beaded bracelet or necklace (if you use a mala, skip over the center bead of attachment) and moving fingers with one bead to the next in coordination with each word adds sensory reprogramming tactics.

Becoming Pliable with Acceptance to Change

An astrologer once told me, "You are going to achieve success by doing it your way." Despite disease and other autoimmune imbalances, I've chosen to free my body and mind, knowing the only one who can do that in this lifetime is little ol' me.

I was unaware of the opportunities awaiting me. Being a one-woman show orchestrating with harmonious chords despite global conversations on constitutional rights, uncovering what was lost provided me a front row ticket to the greatest merry-go-round. As I discovered myself and my path, I made a sincere effort to incorporate love, kindness, and patience into every aspect of my world.

Have you ever noticed how life is like a balancing act? Inter-actions between children and parents, for instance, can be challenging. It requires a delicate touch to ensure everyone feels heard and valued. When we take the time to listen to each other, we can form life-fulfilling bonds. We all have those moments when we know deep down that something is good for us, but we hesitate to leap.

Ladies, are you ready?
Let's take a courageous leap together!

Some women repeatedly express their desire to walk and stretch more consistently but instead only boast of occasional walks to their mailbox or a group fitness class. Others used to workout with a fitness trainer yet today resist action. I can only wonder what it will take for these women to reinstate, upgrade or prioritize their health and wellness fitness routines for positive change.

Do they really want to be flexible in their body and mind? The generations before mine were not as active in fitness; however, creating new habits, though not easy, is doable if we accept the commitment to repattern our psyche.

Where did all the wise women go? Why had so many buried their dreams? Although our joints may stiffen, maintaining wellness vigor is up to the individual by choosing to become pliable in body and mind for the sake of our health's vibrancy. Some moms go head over heels for their children and forget they have a body that needs constant tuning up too.

Is ignoring our inner calling a form of self-denial that hinders graceful aging?

On a sunny June morning, I arrived late to my friend's birthday lunch so I could teach my regular Monday 11:30 yoga class.

Being available to students who, on any given day, might be dealing with fragility in their lives filled me with joy and a sense of purpose. In addition to the physical practice offered by many yoga studios, some communities infuse *bhakti* (love and devotion) and sacred teachings from ancient texts passed down from students to disciples.

After class, a kind-hearted older woman approached me and said, "Marla, we all have a story to share and that's what keeps me ticking."

Her comment assured me that I had made the right decision to teach and double up on my plans for the day.

She proceeded to share intimate details of her current troubles, from body aches to her husband's debilitating health. At that moment, I saw her as a mother, grandmother, wife, and friend going through yet another life phase.

Women serve multiple roles as learners, educators, caregivers, and providers of support in the workplace, public, and with friends and family. Finding solace by relaxing our minds while moving limbs weekly in a class can make for a perfect exchange, where comfort in honoring a piece of our hearts allows us to evaluate our lives with humble grace.

As mentioned, after my mother closed her costume jewelry store, she started to spend more time as a doting grandma. When the grandkids grew up, Mom seemed to have lost her pep. *Had she aged out of reinventing her wheel?* Or, was there still time for her to repurpose her strengths yet again and deal with unresolved losses from her past (including the death of her mother from a heart attack when she was sixteen)?

Vital living requires constant persistence. The Universe provides support. It relies on committed movement with environmental experiences to combat dull aches and fatigue. Sure, we can merely survive – an instinctual initiative beginning the day we are born until we take our last breath. But do we not want to thrive while we are alive? If we fall off our health, wellness, mindfulness track (or were never on it), sitting alone too long with negative thoughts for days or years, our vibrance dulls or sours. Then we must ask ourselves how might we transform, replace void with palpable excitement at every age? If not now, then when?

Our brains can age gracefully by tapping into their reserves, even improving memory loss. Just as lifting weights adds lean muscle to our body, helping us retain muscle later, our brains long to learn new tricks. It takes being silent enough to hear the calls of our intuition. Did we ever want to paint, dance, or sing? Why not sign up for a class? What are you waiting for? Sometimes we have to spice things up to get us out of a rut. Phone a friend you haven't connected with in a while.

Press your fingers at your heart and start tapping them while opening your mouth saying *ahhhhhhhh*.

Proven studies have shown that the majority of people with dementia stopped all formal and informal routes of education in their later years and lacked social connections. Learning something new keeps boredom away and gives us something to look forward to.

Change is inevitable. The Radiant Woman trains her brain with memory recall games. She rejuvenates her cellular body with physical movements to stimulate muscles and nerve endings.

Many children, adults (and even some pets) are suffering at higher rates than ever before from anxiety. Regardless of social status, any use of materialistic or addictive substances leaves us depleted once we come off "the high." Feeling stuffed from excess leaves us afflicted by unfulfilled desires. Even when feeling alone, empty, suffocated, and riddled with bouts of depression, women in pre-, peri-, and post-menopause are also secreting juices to reinvent themselves. They pacify themselves when sad and want to feel joyful even when curveballs are thrown. Life cycle blips and more immense struggles are never going to stop. It is a choice to wander with gloom or bloom with grace.

Managing our emotions, from daily responsibilities to jarring struggles like hormonal changes or unforeseen health issues, zaps our zest unless we focus on breathing intentionally, supporting ourselves and others with nurturing concepts to evolve and grow.

Have we ever wished we could have done things differently, or pursued our dreams instead of conforming to others' expectations? What steps can we take to develop positive habits that reinforce our self-worth? What provisions can we make to produce love and legacy while living in our temporary body? Each of us is woven like a lattice fence, living among each other while mending snags and reconstructing our life stories like patched quilts.

Maintaining our mental health during tender life phases requires persistent upkeep. Mysterious paths will continue to unravel with the people and pets we have cherished and loved.

As we or someone we know reaches old age, we might pray that when it's our time to go, it will be as peaceful as possible.

Perhaps we want to go before our spouse, knowing if they died first life as we knew it would be no more, but rather a bittersweet, unfamiliar end with no limits and rules.

Some have felt abandoned and cooped up; others have been known as "rule followers" or "people pleasers" from good girls to womanhood.

Taking care of our body through stretching connects us with the ethers. Our journey depends on elevating our minds as we ripen with age. While we can take steps to prevent shrinking and smoothen our wrinkles, ultimately, Mother Earth will reclaim us.

Who are we? Where and when will we begin to live knowing that tomorrow it could end?

What is it here that we came to do?

Transforming our unconscious into the superconscious can be achieved by befriending silence as an ally instead of hiding from our past.

Every lifeline milestone offers us an invitation to learn something new. Don't let the impetus slip away!

We can age gracefully by governing our thoughts; rising after we fall; stepping into physical and spiritual radiance as informant operators earning our well-deserved, self-reliant badges; becoming detectives in constant flow of uncovering our hearts and sharing our loving kindness and compassion with others, as in: "*Agent Grace.*"

Whereas I used to favor beer, wine, or tequila, now I prefer mocktails, cacao ceremonies, and chai tea. I have come full circle in my approach to people, bringing all of those I have loved from my past into the future. I have sensed alienation from some but that hasn't stopped me from showing up as I am with people whose opinions and customs differ from mine. I prefer hanging out with radiant beings who elevate one another, sipping the kindness elixir – my sweetest beverage of choice.

When I put my head on the pillow, I want to have sweet dreams, age gracefully into all phases of adulthood with renewed enthusiasm, leave my worries behind, and avoid residue from excessive drinks or harrowing thoughts that can result in unconsciousness or, worse, a hangover headache the next day. This is The Radiant Woman's Way.

Into a New Realm

From tinsel teeth,
to red ribbon dreams;
Growing up,
The creek streams.

Like nesting dolls and secret doors,
Riveting lessons were hidden to be found.
Bitter lemon drops seeped,
my weary eyes abound,

Enduring heartaches,
Earth's sentiments indulging the human race,
for sentient beings are meant to thrive –
trembling waters coexisting with life's fiery base.

Impervious clay, muddled dirt,
sporadic twigs and rubble,

tethered by the winds;
Two dove birds perched on a pergola.

Slender threads of pearly realms,
Meditations' cordial bliss.
Like clamoring noise and silent essentials,
Beckoning life's throne of consciousness.

For if not now, then when will we hear the chimes,
signaling: Our birthright's authentic shine?

Some notice detailed beauty and catch fractions of light that others miss. Slowed-down thoughts invite us to focus on a tree's trunk, bark, branches, limbs, and leaves. Each fragment of discovery can help us access radiance as evolved human beings.

An artist's hand informs through music, dance, poetic spoken or written words, brushstrokes dripping on a canvas, sculptures chiseled, potters molded, or portraits/abstractions graphically designed and photographed. Presentations created for the viewer's entertainment via cinematography, museums, galleries, arenas, halls or concerts have the ability to caress our hearts' brilliance.

When the mind is turbulent, it gets muddy. Yoga practices remind us to keep the waters clear by participating in life. It enables us to love more by identifying the constant love in us as the root of happiness. The body, and what we adorn it in, changes – and so do our thoughts and relationships. Viewpoints change because we keep opening and transforming. What does not change is the sun, with its rises and sets at predictable times. Consider rhythmic intelligence of natural living wisdom to open your intuition.

We were born to move through the chapters, lessons, and healing forces that promote a conscious path – returning to a place of *shakti* (creative feminine energy) rising from the deep place of *kundalini* (yoga of awareness) in the pelvic region, upward toward our heart center to the space of intuition (at the third eye) and into the auric atmosphere. Mantras with specific repetitive sound currents have the potency to raise our bliss state. Implementing tested *Sa Ta Na Ma* mantra formulas has been scientifically proven to prevent and even reverse dementia. The chakra energy systems noted are supplemental and beyond measure.

The Radiant Woman's Way

Adapting to each season of life reminds us to get out of our comfort zones. Being uncomfortable in any phase permits us to grow! Moving your body decreases stress and increases your coordination and communication.

1. **Memory Boost Meditation** (An Alzheimer's Association-approved exercise) intervention/prevention for dementia. It opens your senses through a specific mantra chanted simultaneously with different tonalities and mudra motions for body awareness energy.

   Kirtan (musical reciting); *Kriya* (a cleansing practice influenced by breath sound and movement); *Sa Ta Na Ma Sanskrit* sounds are believed to represent four

lifecycles: birth, life, death, and rebirth. (See appendix
for Sa Ta Na Ma music suggestions. You can also say
the words to the rhythm of "Mary Had a Little Lamb"
for a beat.)

- Sit on a meditation cushion or a chair with both
  feet on the floor.
- Shoulders rolled back.
- With your eyes closed, visualize a looping point
  from the top of the head beaming in and out of the
  frontal lobe, making an L shape with your spine
  elongated.
- Chin in alignment with the earth (to ensure you're
  not leaning head forward or back).
- Use hand gestures with repetition of the sounds to
  shift the chemistry in the brain.
- Place hands on each leg with palms open to coordinate fingers with sounds.
- **Sa** – thumb to forefinger.
- **Ta** – thumb to middle finger.
- **Na** – thumb to ring finger.
- **Ma** – thumb to little finger.
- Using this specified pattern with varied sounds
  and fingers moving alters the brain for higher fre-
  quencies. Repeating the mantra out loud as you
  touch each finger pad with your thumb, first in
  a regular voice, then raising your voice louder,

then in a whisper, and then in silence, creates new neuropathways.

- Studies have shown positive results in reducing dementia by practicing this kriya entirely for 12 minutes daily as a ritual.

- It also serves to induce relaxation, even when used for less time, for anyone.

2. Mantra to Hand Touch Option

Repeat "I am thank-ful" as you touch your thumb to each finger:

- **I** – Thumb to forefinger
- **am** – Thumb to middle finger
- **thank** – Thumb to ring finger
- **ful** – Thumb to little finger

Each human experience gives us a chance to connect to cosmic energies. Connections are gifts from the Universe.

Journal Prompt

Begin today by writing a passion/vision statement. Reacquaint yourself with purpose, reclaim your powerful presence, calm inflammation, and spread your wings to fly.

Chapter 10

THE GIFT OF ADVENTURE THROUGH THE ART OF RADIANCE

"The biggest adventure you can take is to live the life of your dreams."

~ Oprah Winfrey

One ordinary rainy afternoon in Great Britain stands out. Despite the dismal weather, I flourished and set out for an adventure for a loosely mapped-out spring break excursion. I took a train from Bradford to London, met up with a new acquaintance, and went by ferry from the wet docks to sunny Athens – a historical city known for its ancient ruins. The travel adrenaline, though exhausting, had me feeling more alive than ever.

Let's Go Europe, widely known as the bible of guidebooks for budget-conscious travelers, offered spot-on tips for hopping from one country or town to another. It mapped out day trips with lodging, meals and sightseeing suggestions, steering young adults and students backpacking through cities, many living their bohemian dreams with minimal luggage or purpose.

Upon arriving in Greece at night, we made a deal as *Let's Go* suggested and hitched a ride with a semi-trailer truck driver en route to Athens. It was noted that the journey by eighteen-wheeler would take five hours. After munching on a banana and some snacks from our driver, we trusted the process – making small talk about where we were from, had traveled, and what we would explore while in Greece. We drifted asleep in the surprisingly roomy space behind the trucker's cab seat. It was, after all, designed for transporters to nap. He would be driving straight through, with no other stops or deliveries. Worked for us!

Though I felt safe, I clearly remember thinking, *If only my parents knew where I slept tonight…* (Maybe this will come as a shocker to some of you reading this now!)

I woke up to a magnificent highway sunrise and soon after, we reached our destination, excited to get acclimated in the first of our youth hostels amidst cobblestone squares. Our accommodations ensured us easy access to exploration. My instant observance of city life was of its loud commotion. Yet, the noise dissipated once I connected to other travelers and locals of similar ages from different parts of the world. I felt accepted and embraced by many.

Athens felt like a home away from home in a few short days.

Once our accents were revealed, conversations naturally went to the USA. Small-talk opinions arose about the American government and President Ronald Reagan. People I met at local cafes first assumed I was of Greek descent due to my chestnut hair and slightly olive-toned skin.

This kind of chatter continued for a week until it was time to leave behind the cafes, the Acropolis, and the Parthenon and board another ferry bound for Mykonos. Following our handy guidebook again, we planned to hitchhike to our next hostel. We walked a few miles from the dock on a scorching dusty road. My backpack, stuffed by then with collectibles, weighed me down. With each cumbersome step, I hoped someone would pick us up since road activity, like at the dock, had been infrequent. After being thumbs-up for almost an hour, we finally hopped into a man's pickup truck. Winding cobblestone streets, adorned with floral terraces, windowpanes, and sills on white stucco villas, settled my overzealous mood. Everything felt bright and expansive. I shed more armor and traded it in for laid-back island living.

I imbued great wealth by pursuing my studies abroad at a subsidized university instead of a more popular American program. Without an entourage of travelers or having a best friend near for the onset and duration of my time away, I had to make new friends and succumb to peers, where I felt uncomfortable. The aloneness of being solo with no one to turn to except myself strengthened me.

My free-spirited nature exploded. I no longer waited to be invited to frat parties nor fretted over what to wear at Studio 54 in New York City. Life back home became a distant memory.

The tangible, interactive education brought me into a world of diverse cultures and languages. Hands-on experiences impressed me way more than book smarts.

In England, my peer students cued me on their accents and dialects. I learned the distinction between proper Londoners, with their city status, and the countrified south and industrial working class of northern parts of the country. The infamous fish (lightly battered) n' chips (french fries salted with vinegar) were the great unifiers in pub establishments, along with proper teatime enjoyed by all.

Though I knew it existed, my life was filled with less social drama – with no parents or friends to report to or console. Each place I landed led me to figure things out for myself, even if it was simply the currency exchange rate in each country. (At the time, the dollar was worth a good amount in exchange for the British pound.)

As my travels neared their end in late April, I booked a last-minute open-ended flight to Paris. Arriving alone in the city of love, I chose to stay in a hotel instead of a hostel – a splurge before I headed home.

I had picked an area on the outskirts of this city, thinking it would be a great, central location to visit various sites. No wonder the price was so reasonable, I soon noticed! After a day of touring and dinner, I discovered I was in the red-light district, where activity from hustlers escalated at night. That sealed my decision to leave that part of town first thing in the morning. The following small hotel was filled with businesspeople.

On that second day, I set out to cover as many spots on the map as possible. I explored The Louvre, waiting in line to see the much-smaller-than-expected *Mona Lisa* and many other exquisite paintings. I then moved into a small, single bedroom in a comfortable hostel for a third night to keep things on a budget. I felt at home as I turned the key into my door after touring for four more "final" nights (remember, my ticket was open-ended). I was alone without a buddy by my side, yet alive and well in a city I had come to love and know quite well by the time I left.

My extended stay allowed me to peruse Montmartre – a magnificent masterpiece vivid from afar and quite splendid up close. It was a whimsical art culture, rich with high energy, in the world's most romantic city.

A spectacular staircase to the massive white dome of Sacre-Coeur church invites tourists to sit, eat, converse, and people-watch. It leads to a charmed square full of bustling artists selling paintings, including on-the-spot portraits. From every angle, the scene high on a hill took my breath away, evoked joy, and brought me to tears as I observed families and individuals shopping, eating, conversing and engaging amongst their travel companions, couples, groups, and families from afar.

Watching artists in action, their easels out as they interacted with tourists eager to paint portraits, ignited a revelation in me. I later understood why I was forever changed after hanging out for five long hours, followed by a subsequent visit. The place I was so drawn to was where Picasso, Miro and, before them, Manet and Van Gogh painted and called their home.

I was living on a student budget, stretching my money in those final weeks to make new memory impressions. Soon after arriving at my university for the semester, I investigated finding a job so I didn't have to tap into my savings or worry about spending. Attaining the appropriate working papers in a foreign country was a challenging task. Each day was less about frills and more about maturing, personal growth, and adventure. It felt wonderous to be alive. On that day, as the sun went down, I ate another baguette with thinly shaved cheese, observing diners at open-air cafes while I sat on a curb. Captivated by the supreme energy at dusk, I thought, *I hope to visit with someone I love one day.*

Money issues aside, my extended stay allowed me to walk over bridges and through parks, use public transportation, check out nook-and-cranny floral balusters and terraces, circle highlighted Paris landmarks on a map, and navigate around the Seine River.

"*Café au lait, s'il vous plaît,*" was my mantra.

As I awaited my order and long after I finished, I would overhear neighboring conversations. That is when I developed a keen appetite for indulging in new savory tastes to satisfy and heighten my palette and the happy-go-lucky experience of people watching. I loved noting this European world around me and fancied an imagined trip to France again someday (with funds to appreciate its finer gourmet cuisine).

Before I knew it, it was time to swap the Parisian allure with dazzling couture for traditional English tea and toast and finish my academic program. Dorm life and life, in general, could have been more fanciful in Bradford, England, including the mediocre food in the dining hall.

Breakfast choices were bleak for my American sensibilities, but one cereal was the infamous "*Weetabix*" (a three-inch, oval-shaped, biscuit-like wheat formation that dissolved in milk). It was new to me and quite delightful, as was the shepherd's pie – a staple comfort food of whipped mashed potatoes, savory beef, and peas encapsulated by baker's crust. I fancied "Maltesers," light confectioner's chocolate malt balls that melted in my mouth.

It was also in England that I was introduced to the tantalizing flavors and seasonings found in Indian cuisine. Many years later, during my hatha yoga training, I again fell in love with cumin and curry.

Ready, Set, Go

How did I get myself into this predicament? I thought as I peered out at a mist of white clouds.

Earlier that morning, Jonathan and I had hopped into a navy Chevy Tahoe truck and set out on a fifty-minute drive from northern New Jersey to "The Ranch" in Hudson Valley, New York. The crisp morning air recharged my senses as a blue jay squawked, squirrels frolicked, and a deer family pranced by, with one staring intensely at us from the wooded lot surrounding the driveway. It was the fall of 1996, and our babysitter from around the block had arrived to watch over our two little ones while we were gone.

Hubby was all set to redeem the sky-diving certificate I had gifted him for his thirty-third birthday. Upon reaching The Ranch, we ascended the steps of a trailer and entered a dank, brown-paneled modular building site. As he registered for the dive, I thought of my parents and in-laws, who had no idea what he was about to do.

While inside, the woman at the counter asked if I was also going skydiving. Though I never imagined myself doing so, I said yes! On a tandem skydive jump, the trained partner uses a parachute built for two people. The jump is made from 13,500 feet, weather permitting, and from there, you freefall.

First, we watched a video demonstration in a room full of other participants, then signed our lives away via waivers and agreements. Next, we put on jumpsuits, gladiator boots, and other equipment and gadgets to lock in with our tandem partner.

I remember walking with the group to the tarmac, the spiral fresh in my mind. Impulsive felt right. I was safe and invincible, especially with my outdoorsy, midwestern husband by my side.

Then I remembered I would be attached to a stranger during the jump.

Two groups went out from two different planes. As we walked up the plank into the unlit cabin of the ten-seater aircraft, it appeared eerie and deserted even being filled up. It was far different from the usual commercial jetliners I was accustomed to in my travels.

I put my seatbelt on, and then we went up, up, and away, soaring into the sky for a quick ride.

My ears popped as the noisy engine roared, the airplane throttling through the air. Seatbelts unlatched amid the organized chaos, and, two by two, paying participants and their tandem partners began to rise, ready for the adventure ahead.

I began to sweat. Felt a bit woozy. Not only had I just signed my life away, but I was also now handing my life over to a stranger.

Feeling alone even though I would be transcending with another, I did my best to release the surge of rising tension. I felt scared when my tandem partner grabbed me close to his clamp and hooked me up to him.

Then it was my turn. As I walked to the ledge and peered out the aircraft, anxiety rose within me. Though it felt strange to watch others fly knowing I'd soon be next, I gathered courage and made a conscious decision not to let my nerves get the best of me. There was no turning back or room to hesitate. Before second-guessing, I took the plunge. Ready or not, jump!

I did not love the freezing cold wind against my cheeks. The clouds were distant. Were they above or below me as I tried to get my bearings? I opened my arms wide. *Look at me; I can fly like the birds!* I thought with a gushing adrenaline rush, releasing all worries and fears... until I searched for Jonathan.

Where was he in the sky?

Everyone had their arms out spinning while a videographer (if you hired one, and we did) flew from one tandem group to another, capturing our playful antics. In one glimpse I went numb, though I turned my thumbs up to let my guide know I was okay.

While freefalling, I regained composure with intense precision in awe of the vast, breathtaking sky. Being up so high transported me onto another timeline. Exhilaration entered my energy field. In a split second, all tension was released, like in meditation. Just as quickly came my wish for a safe landing. Flying was magical and scary. I had done it, my only jump, and could now retire.

Later, my friend Ilene and Mom exclaimed. "I can't believe you both went up on the same plane! What if it crashed? The kids would have been orphans."

I wasn't afraid for the most part – and true to my nature. And I have continued to live with intuitive spontaneity when trying something new.

Transitioning via one excursion to the next while trusting my instincts when meeting someone for the first time or approaching an unfamiliar setting came naturally.

Being spontaneous has advantages, as it can allow us to live a bit untamed life. Not second-guessing my decisions or over-thinking has served me well. I've often had the opportunity to live in flow rather than in fear.

Throughout my life, when faced with an adrenalin-releasing experience – even a scary one – I've had a motto that helps me move magically and gracefully through it. As my father always said, "Don't waste your time worrying since ninety-nine percent of the time, all will be well."

I Am Brave

I carried cumbersome equipment for a scuba dive to roam the ocean's murky depths. After an abbreviated intro session due to the cruise line's late tender schedule, it was time to jump in.

In an instant, I went numb. The group's presence left me with no choice but to kick my fins. Proud for not allowing fright to get in my way of adventure, I gave my thumbs up to signal the guide that I was okay. Mission accomplished.

Though I preferred venturing with my feet on land over jumping from the sky and diving under waves, "At least I tried."

By playing it safe, we might miss out on thrilling experiences. Cold showers, plunges, cryotherapy, or ice baths might not feel great, but we do so for the benefit of shutting down our organs to rejuvenate our cellular bodies. When we encounter a challenge that excites us but also scares us, it's important to proceed cautiously while inviting our inner wisdom. Even if we fail to accomplish our goal, the experience can lead us to discover another passion - a new sport, academic pursuit, or art form. It can open our eyes to deeper passions and opportunities.

And that's what happened when a retired childhood sport got an overhaul – thanks to a neighbor's positive influence. Being on the road with cars and other more advanced bikers was scary, but pedaling connected me to my inner child. Being surrounded by nature increased my awareness. After a few local charity bike rides, I signed up for a more intense one to benefit those with multiple sclerosis. Little did I know that one of my friends would reroute us, turning the twenty-five miles we had registered for to fifty. Also, my wider wheels kept me at a disadvantage compared to other streamlined bikes and experienced riders. At some point, feeling completely depleted, I wanted to quit. Yet I persevered even when it felt like I could no longer pedal.

Pedaling to the end was a remarkable feat, likened to the births of my children. I gained confidence and strength. Before the ride, I took to the hills of my neighborhood for months. In the days leading up to the event, I proudly raised money and awareness for the MS Foundation. When the ride became overbearing, I considered opting out, hopping into a van to finish; instead, I stayed on my bike to the main events finishing room. Many bikers collapsed, got chair massages. People in wheelchairs, family, friends, and some who had walked a bit cheered us on.

As time went on, the rigors and dangers of biking outdoors (I once tipped over onto the road after locking my feet into the pedals), my allergies during hay fever and ragweed season, and my neurological tingles led me to trade my bike for a yoga mat. I offered my body what was needed to relax. The movement and peaceful stimuli quieted my mind.

I remembered my first instructor, Anna from Sweden. Her demeanor was calm, lean, and serene. I wanted more. That early memory of peace stayed with me. A decade later, I further experimented with its physical practice.

The more I delved into my heart and sensations became entangled, the more I released congested stuff that had been bottled up inside of me for years. My steadfast meditation and self-development allowed me to further sense my soul's untouched, pure depth. It allowed me to climb the ladder, profoundly reach myself by never giving up hope.

Years later, when my family and I climbed Machu Picchu, I wanted to stop. Many other older and younger tourists chose to wait it out on the side and quit. My oldest daughter, Amanda, took my hand in hers. She patiently cheered me on as I hiked up the many uneven stone steps. She waited for me and I made it! Support from a mentor, friend, coach, or family member can help us overcome painful moments when we want to give up on our pursuit. In the end it's up to us to decide if we want to get over the humps of life to reach the finish line!

Fast Forward to the Pandemic

Over the days, then weeks, of the lockdown, I cautiously observed my thoughts.

Though worry crossed my mind, I challenged myself to focus on what I could do to help my family, parents, in-laws, friends, aunts and uncles, cousins, students, teachers, and the world.

Despite the ever-changing storms of life,
a Radiant Woman shines by redirecting her internal
conversation toward bliss.

When rapid changes occur outside us, we can meditate on serenity and bring calm into our cellular bodies. Splashing in water, literally and figuratively, can invoke positive energy feedback, painting a newer, harmonious color picture in all walks of life.

Since sitting near or in the rubbish of our minds distracts us, we can switch our inner landscape to have the experience of a lifetime. It might not be sky/scuba diving, rock climbing, or snorkeling, but self discovery also keeps our adrenaline going; its greatest reward is in the transformation. Withstanding resistance gives us wings to elevate our mood.

The human brain is one of, if not the, most powerful "computers" of them all. The Radiant Woman maintains hers before it crashes. The human body's intricate wiring was built to operate smoothly as we explore soothing and perhaps daring depths. Any human who wants to get closer to radiance takes the initiative to reprogram their mind through dynamic, energetic, peaceful, meditative intricacies; they may seem to others like they've entered encrypted formulas.

Motivation and inspiration come from inside-out and outside-in.

Our brain also tends to keep us safe, comfortable, and secure; thus, it will talk us out of anything we want to do to stay out of harm's way – even if the risk has the potential to be good for us. So why not stand proud, roll our shoulders back, mingle with nature and anything that excites or frustrates us by using emotions as inspirational fuel? Commit to self-care!

It is up to us to feel fulfilled when our heads hit the pillow at the end of the day. The actions we take, friendships we make, families we live with and create, and hobbies we explore throughout our lives affect everyone with whom we're in a relationship. I hungered for self-love/care where love was like money, an energy moving from one hand to another.

The Radiant Woman embraces courage in her unique way. She rolls her shoulders back, lifts her chin in alignment with the Earth and away from the endless scroll on the phone. She seeks ways to fill in the gaps and *missing links* in her life to discover and uncover her innate natural radiance. Use your imagination to take a new route, be it by public or personal transportation, to a familiar park, town, state or country. Go to the places you have been with fresh eyes or travel somewhere you've never been to. The point is to get out of your comfort zone.

There's a difference between noting an initial mental and or physical ailment, intuitively listening to your body, and following up by taking action to manage related emotions when healing. No matter the struggle, each experience requires a new frequency to alter a prior automatic response. All recovery influences our future. There's growth in learning or trying something new.

The Radiant Woman's Way

Digging into compass directions – North, South, East, and West – reveals the depths and heights of your life's exploration.

Self-love Balance Practice

1. Find a comfy spot to take a few breaths.
   - Close your eyes if that feels okay for you (or let a little light in).
   - Breathe in the ocean of awareness, exhale the sweet wisdom of the world.
   - Imagine flying, soaring high, maintaining optimal health and healing through adventure.
   - Inhale: vast oceans.
   - Exhale: infinite sky.
   - Repeat for 1–3 breaths.
   - Sit in silence for a few moments after.

2. What ventures or excursions can you plan for today, this week, month or year to help you connect with your heart space? Note: this self-discovery exploration doesn't require a faraway destination; bliss is acquired by turning the dial in a new direction to transpose the scenery of your mind.

- Get a real or imaginary pen and journal or type in the note section of your phone.

- Declare in one powerful statement what being a Radiant Woman means to you.

- Write down a past adventure that brought you joy and radiance.

Observe your body in silence for a few moments.

Chapter 11

SEARCHING FOR LOVE WITHIN

"Another person is not responsible for our happiness because when we are alone, we are whole. Whole, perfect and effulgent."

~ Sheryl Edsall

A late bloomer in uncovering some of my hidden passions, I went to college undecided. By sophomore year, even though sociology was my favorite class and where I met my next year's roommate, I followed my father's recommendation (or perhaps what I felt most adept at) and became a business major.

Embarking solo to a foreign country took perky courage as I lugged one massive black suitcase. When navigating from one unfamiliar place to another I learned to follow my instincts with caution, figure things out, and follow maps with naive contentment.

Those early musings, meanderings, and wanderings set my travel wheels in locomotion. The compacted nine-month junior year abroad not only transformed my mind with newfound beauty, it opened me to an opulence I had never imagined.

Eating alone in cafes initiated my first "dating myself" experiences. Instead of waiting for plans to surface, I made my timeline. It felt liberating. My search for a boyfriend/future husband went on standby.

When it was time to come home, I gave Mom and Dad a fright because I didn't want to leave my destination. In my final months away, I had joined a *Kibbutz* community in Israel, living off the land. While there, I picked watermelons under a scorching sun, sorted and labeled audio reels, and assisted in the kitchen preparing recipes in large vats. My life was open-ended until I booked my return flight to America. During that pivotal transition home, I brought a fresh and visionary perspective.

Upon reflection, my time abroad was significant because it piqued my curiosity for understanding human interactions beyond the material world.

In 1988, I graduated from The University of Rhode Island with a Bachelor of Science in Marketing. Many great opportunities were on the horizon. I spent those final summer days waiting tables at The Coast Guard House in Narragansett – a beach town near my university – then returned home to my family's English Tudor in the New Jersey suburbs. Its brick exterior was charmingly covered with cascading ivy, reminiscent of the homes I saw in England.

My final business paper was a structured marketing plan for opening an art-influenced gallery. After meandering in Europe the year prior, I dreamed of a fanciful boutique filled with eclectic tastes where I would travel worldwide to find unique merchandise to showcase.

Unlike my business peers, upon graduation, I took a different route. The majority joined large companies in corporate America. I decided not to follow that lane after my family's experience with antisemitism (see blog - Glossary). Despite being qualified, my dad was denied a VP position meant for him due to his Jewish faith. After a lengthy legal battle, it was found that the company had violated anti-discrimination laws. Prejudice due to misguided hierarchy systems and misnomers put his profession and our family's financial stability on hold.

To this day, Dad says he was grateful for that rocky road because it gave him direction to pursue another career. He brought the sales and district manager team skills he had learned earlier, along with his jovial enthusiasm to serve others, into building a new vision. For me, it was a tough lesson to absorb, but it gave me a reason to hold onto my dream of becoming an independent entrepreneur someday.

I was prudent in not wanting to follow a corporate route. While scanning the "help wanted" newspaper section, my eyes caught sight of a job that didn't require my college degree. I applied and interviewed anyway; thus, my first post-college position was as an art associate in an international gallery that housed everything from traditional paintings, prints, sculptures, and "wearable art" fine jewelry that needed to be placed in a safe at closing to abstract pieces. Their vast collection ranged from Erte lithographs to Norman Rockwell drawings to Disney animation cels (pre-digital). Fritz Freeling's Pink Panther and other cartoon original artists are highly sought after and collectible. I sold many techno-color treasures, which are also known as dying art.

Falling in love while going outside of the box contributed to the timelessness aspect of my dating myself. The more we encourage learning at any phase, training muscle memory as we grow, the more we enliven our purpose. This came to me many years later in my self-awareness and transcendence in womanhood.

From squirming in cribs to rolling out of bed, entering one door, closing another, we revolutionize the flame of uncertainty with faith. Shoe tying permits us to become our gatekeepers, and discipline opens our hearts' forces with each trial and error. It moves us to deflect what we're meant to repel – churning the burn of uncomfortableness by turning keys toward love. Each valiant beam becomes a catalyst for redirection if we listen to our gut intuition. When we welcome all aspects of incompleteness into our inner and outer circles, we allow our raw truth to expand so we love ourselves before searching for a partner in any arena of life, be it in family, business, or intimate relationships.

Many girls turned women from my generation and prior were programmed by parents, news, magazines, and TV or authoritarian figures to look outward for love and acceptance from others. (In some ways, this continues today.)

My life became unhinged when frustration, worry, or negativity clogged my mind. What was I looking for?

What are you looking for?

Who was I then? Was I good enough now? What might our futures look like as we move into womanhood – be it as a mentor, friend, wife, sister, aunt or mom? I had yet to learn who or what my purpose was, but if I had limited myself long ago, I may never have uncovered the artist in me.

Old business cards remained tucked away in the back of my desk drawer. Each title reminded me of a different frame in my life: art associate to sales and marketing rep. There was a gap until my yoga classes and gift business, "Aspire with Marla," came to fruition.

The more I followed my breath and observed my thoughts, the more I noticed how I could interrelate with others before reacting from the perceptions of my mind. When I instead operate from a pure, intentional heart, The Radiant Woman inside of me no longer longs to be accepted.

I was thrilled when Naturally Yoga, my beloved home away from home, opened its groovy, delicious, vegetarian Nectar Café to serve the health-conscious community. From various soups and salads to cold-pressed juices, customers were greeted with aromatic flair. The lime-green walls and prayer flags, believed to bring happiness, peace, prosperity, good fortune, health, and victory, invited the community into their sacred space. A purple Buddha sat on the dome-cased stainless-steel refrigerator countertop while cool musical tunes played. The soulful staff's hospitable attention nourished me before I ate.

One day, Neil Edsall, one of my meditation teachers, was behind the counter. He is married to Sheryl, co-owner of the yoga studio and, at that time, the cafe.

"Happy birthday," I said, ordering two sweet potato empanadas and a jambalaya soup.

After enjoying each morsel in the cozy backroom, which had five tables, plants, and an antique wooden bench, I settled the bill and bid Neil farewell with warm wishes.

"Will you be celebrating with your other half later today?"

"Thank you, dear," he replied, then added, "And yes, though to be clear, Sheryl's not my other half as I am complete all by myself. I don't need someone else to make me full."

"Ahha…" I replied.

I was introduced to this concept during my first year of teacher training. It was anchored in our group's visit to Ananda Ashram with Naturally Yoga, a gift from the studio after our required exams. There, I received another gift in the form of a new mantra.

I am whole, perfect as I am (Om Punrnam Adah). ~ A Vedic Upanishad from Hindu scripture

I fell in love with this mantra as soon as I began chanting it. The translation spoke to me with a soulful realization that words cannot describe.

Finding a love partner to complete me had been instilled in me by societal influences from Hallmark cards to Hollywood movies to magazines. Re-remembering who I was again was a vital part of the stripping-down process that led me to untethered spaces, sacred places. The love I had for humanity also included myself in the equation. I am complete and don't need anyone else to fill me up. While it's important to interact and complement each other, loving oneself is crucial to success in all relationships.

We can strengthen our existence if we understand that we were born perfect, needing only to meld with our higher self. We can reprogram our minds by welcoming the guru (remover of darkness) into our relationships. If we stripped away the need to meet our "other half" to be fulfilled, what might we discover about the wondrous people we know (including ourselves) and others we have yet to meet?

I am enough,
you are enough,
we are enough.
Together we climb, fall, and vibrate in love with the
cosmos.

What can you do today to fill yourself up with more meaningful love?

When was the last time you went on a date with yourself? The concept helped me flip the way I had been brought up to meet a man, get married, and live happily ever after.

Once the fairytale romance ends (after the honeymoon phase), we get into the crux of our relationships. No level of income or health can bring us fierce love if fear burdens us.

A yogic lifestyle unites togetherness. Observing, not over-reacting, and reframing before complaining enhances our communication. Switching gears when detours arise leads to love, commitment, and acceptance.

Compassion is a gift from the heart.

The Radiant Woman chooses self-exploration to calm and energize herself on command to share her best version with others.

Re-engaging emotional stability and mental clarity can lead to a renewed sense of enchantment, whether stepping onto a train or climbing a steep trail at any stage of life.

Self-reliance and guidance from love and nature give modern women tools to channel spiritual connections. By melding ancient wisdom, depth perception, and mind–body fitness, we can ignite our intuitive, unfiltered passions to guide us.

Symbolism

Every fraction of light assumes its position due to the relativity and projection from brilliant *Suriya* (Sanskrit for sun) and lunar *chandra* (Sanskrit for moon). Each person's molecules uniquely represent nature's mysteries, like an unpredictable weather forecast with a mind of its own. We can elevate our higher selves by anticipating our bright future by giving our undivided attention to disrupting negative habitual patterns.

In other words, you make a secret pact to care for yourself by prioritizing peace.

Pure love mirrors our reflection in nature. The sun shines her brilliance back at us. A juicy orange's flesh opens our taste buds with bursting energy.

The Radiant Woman's Way
Dating

1. What might a date with yourself feel, look, taste, smell, or sound like? Write it out, including your five senses. Imagine the scene. Schedule time for yourself on your calendar! Set an alarm and don't break your date.

2. *Reiki* is a peaceful, non-invasive self-care regimen you can add before bed to calm down or any time of day to explore the concept of dating (being in a relationship with) yourself.

   You can try these hand positions reclining in bed at night or on a couch or chair. Relax and recline to connect and unwind.

   - Place both hands on the crown of your head, visualize light flowing, and breathe.
   - Place one hand on your forehead and one on your heart. Visualize light flowing, and breathe.
   - Place one or both hands on your chest at your heart center. Visualize light flowing and breathe.

- Keep one hand at the heart center, place one on your abdomen, visualize light flowing, and breathe.

- Place both hands on your abdomen, visualize light flowing, and breathe.

Accept yourself as you are in this moment. Embrace your own unique and gentle warmth. Shift hand positions when you feel ready to.

- Practice for 1–3 minutes (no need for a timer).

- Relax, play, and use the hand positions in any arrangement, anytime.

Chapter 12

STAYING RADIANT IN OUR RELATIONSHIPS, FROM SPIRIT GUIDES, ANGELS, AND SAINTS TO SENTIENT BEINGS

"Wherever you are, and whatever you do, be in love."

~ Rumi

I recall the time I rang my friend's doorbell and her husband asked if we were heading to a pep rally for the same team. I understood the joke immediately because of our red shirts and black pants. We could have chosen denim or a different color top; instead, unbeknownst to us, we had gotten the extraterrestrial memo, a telepathy friendship message.

Vanessa and I met soon after she moved around the block from me and quickly we became great friends. A natural leader, she formed our book club that exists to this day, though it's now primarily virtual. What began as a club for the newcomers later led to a spin-off to keep some of "the regulars" in a smaller, more intimate circle.

Our kids shared Halloween celebrations, birthday parties, old-fashioned rhymes, Tonka trucks, Madame Alexander dolls and tea parties. We shared a mutual love for *The Nutcracker* and *Swan Lake*, and, of course, reading – from *Devil in the White City*, a true story about a serial killer set during the building of the Chicago World's Fair in 1893, to *City of Dreams*, a work of historical fiction set against the backdrop of seventeenth century Manhattan ("then New Amsterdam"), including the medical practices and apothecaries of the time.

Sometimes, Vanessa and I drove aimlessly around neighboring towns to explore. We would comment on certain homes with charming characteristics. Creatures of habit, we routinely got lost after hitting one infamous dead-end that sprung from winding streets near our friend's house on Hickory Trail. Our sense of direction (or lack thereof) never failed to evoke laughter.

Though similar in many ways, we had many differences too. Vanessa's orderly manner complimented my laid-back, easygoing nature. On many occasions, I watched her receive a beautiful wedding invitation or baby announcement in the mail, write the date and details in her calendar, and quickly proceed to throw the paper, even if engraved, out. In contrast, I had cluttered corkboards and piled papers on my desk. I never seemed to get ahead of my clutter while she'd get rid of what was no longer needed without attachment. When she came to my home office, she'd help me organize by filling hefty green bags.

Hmm, was I a hoarder? What was I holding onto?

I had an endless supply of saved correspondences, little motivations written on scrap paper and even a nightgown my mom gave me from her wedding night in a little storage box, plus *tchotchkes* (little knickknack collectibles) galore.Vanessa's motto long before organizer influencers came into play was: "Everything has a shelf life and expiration date. It gets the boot if you haven't used it in six months!"

A lover of nature, animals, and flowers, Vanessa created the most beautiful fairy gardens and intricate decorative needlepoints. Our friendship fed off one another like a grandiose complement; each season of life's rotations fed our souls, as did our love for the annual holiday cookie exchange. Her glittered pink and green snowflake sugar cookies with their buttery appeal and classic décor were perfection. Each year, mouths watered in anticipation of Sue's tantalizing gingerbread cookie. One year, the three of us gathered to make the batter, roll the dough, cut, bake, and bag before our traditional gathering. My twice-baked chocolate chip oatmeal biscotti was also loved by many. Our shared passions went beyond the scope of gourmet to conventional recipes, nature, and entertainment.

We'd sip our mutual favorite Earl Grey tea while discussing everything from what was happening in our children's lives at school and extracurricular activities to who was cooking what for dinner. We rehashed stories that shaped our lives and challenges our daughters encountered by "mean girls," and we discussed shared values we instilled in our sons and daughters that celebrated old-fashioned roots in modern times.

I could tell her anything from my discomfort and tingles in my fingers and toes to what was going on with any one of my kids' learning abilities, be it on the playfields, dance or gymnastic floors, or classrooms.

Then Vanessa got sick. She followed doctors' recommendations for ten years, recovering from procedures that left her lethargic and limp, yet she willed hard to get better. In that way, Vanessa never gave up hope or complained.

I recall helping Vanessa select paint from a Benjamin Moore rolodex sample color wheel for her bathroom walls. Yellow appeared much brighter than you expected, so I recommended a soothing mellow yellow, thinking it preferable to an overly stimulating shade that would bounce off her porous walls.

Each time I entered Vanessa's house, it was full of cheer. Always pristine and set up for the holidays.

When I visited her in February 2020 with a Valentine in hand, I was surprised to see she had not had any heart décor yet. I thought this was not like her; the holiday was approaching.

Their brick red walls, golden yellow kitchen cabinetry, and Biedermeier furniture were enhanced by art. Some walls were adorned with captivating originals bought at auction; one Miro stroked the core of my heart.

Her soulmate partnered with Vanessa for love and was full of devotion all the while my dear friend dealt with her health challenges. His persona was calm, kind, and intelligent; he was also known (by those around town who were lucky enough to be invited over for a meal) as a top-notch, self-taught chef.

He frequented the grocery store, buying the freshest ingredients. A well-rounded, humble man who took each of Vanessa's doctor visits in stride and afterward formulated emails to friends and family with optimistic and forthcoming reports, he also "researched on his own," as Vanessa said.

In her final years after brain surgery to release pressure from the cancer that had spread, she no longer drove but sat on the couch near her kitchen unless friends or family took her out.

During one visit, after I spent the morning preparing lunch, I served us salad with fennel and radishes. That's when I found out she disliked the latter, but at least I knew she didn't like flaky coconut like my youngest daughter.

After decades, I still have much to learn about my beautiful friend; I thought as I saw her decline, including imbalance and slowed speech, right before my eyes.

Painkillers took the edge off her stomach and other discomforts, but then she felt "loopy." One day she cried while we discussed our mothers.

"Sometimes it's hard to talk to them on the phone," we agreed.

I shared why I avoided calling my mom before teaching or taking yoga classes. I wanted my mind to be a clear channel of grace, and certain communications messed with my head. I tried to detach from drama and bring my intuitive mind to the mat. Vanessa too avoided calling her mom, but for entirely different reasons. She did not want her mom to be saddened when her health worsened. That's when she cried.

Why was I plating lunch for us in her kitchen? I wished she was the one serving me rather than being sick. I observed her head and shoulders slumped one notch while seated on her fruit chintzes patterned seat cushion tied on a high back slatted wooden chair.

"Where is the olive oil?" I asked.

She then directed me to a cabinet above her wall oven as I heated soup on her Viking stovetop. Its powerful gas flame lit up harmoniously. Not only was her traditional décor beautiful, but it was well-designed and functional – the scene of so many shared meals that she and her husband seasoned with memory filled moments for their children, friends and family to enjoy.

Though Vanessa received additional nutrition assistance from a tube to keep her strong, she still had a distinguished palette for seasoning and flavors while nibbling and eating slowly. She remarked on her love for the "smooth texture" of the soup I had made us for lunch. After that, I went to prepare a plate of dessert cookies.

"No thanks, my stomach hurts and has cramped up again. It's probably from all the medication," she replied.

The pain in the head turned bad later that same day. I sensed she wasn't ever going to get better.

She cried again.

I left that day feeling glad that at least she felt safe enough to speak of her heartache and shed tears with me. I also feared the day she'd lose her voice or ability to move in her graceful ways. I prayed she'd beat the cancer out of her cells. She'd had some wonderful years after her initial diagnosis ten years prior. This time around, it seemed like her body was no longer capable of recouping; it had slowed down, withering as we all watched with dismay.

I couldn't fathom being in her shoes. It felt awful to witness her moving into a graver phase. All hope lost. No treatment plan to remedy or control what was happening.

Her life was sheer translucence and no longer resembled a life of living. She'd lounge on a rust-colored sectional couch in her living room staring at beautiful art with fingers no longer nimble enough for her beloved needlecraft. She gazed through the windows of nature while her days had turned into a bore.

As pertinent info and dates slipped her mind, Vanessa exclaimed that she was in a fog. She also forgot what happened in a book soon after finishing it.

On an earlier visit, I noticed her needlepoint projects were no longer in her kitchen.

Where did the amazing apparatus magnifiers go for her refined detail? Before leaving for a few errands, her hubby reminded Vanessa to heat the pad in the microwave to help her fingers from stiffening up because they'd been cramping at night with painful spasms. One day, she got confused when her daughter joked about her whereabouts (to make matters more confusing, she lived across the country). Her brain wasn't processing information in a way that recognized humor. I wanted there to be a surgery or remedy drug to undo her pain. To renew her brain and relax her three cramped fingers so everything could be okay.

In my first writers' group, which started seven months before the pandemic, I listened intently as one woman shared an excerpt. Her piece described the death of a loved one living out her final days on a bed in their family room. They held hands. This image struck a chord with me because it was exactly what I thought about.

I didn't even know if I would get to see my friend in the end. Vanessa stopped visitors from visiting her in her bedroom, whenever she had been sequestered as her health worsened. She kept that space private and holy.

A few years prior, we had visited Janet, a mutual friend with whom I had shared many cookie exchanges and yoga classes, who was dying from cancer. It was the first time I was in the presence of someone who was transitioning. Janet's eyes spoke with love up until the very end. Her family appreciated our visit. We were a distraction from her final farewell. At Janet's funeral, Vanessa wore a colorful scarf, saying, "It was important to brighten the scenery." Vanessa loved life and was graceful in every way.

At her house before and during those first months of the pandemic, I gave Vanessa hugs and let her cry in front of me, yet she was alone with her discomfort. Again, she had already gone through years of gradual decline as she followed the doctor's orders. They did a decent job, and I am grateful for her extended years of life. On the other hand, was it a crime to put poison in to kill off the cancer beast? For sure we all thought she would survive, like her mother, who had beat the same genetic cancer.

In Vanessa's case, remnants of diseased cells multiplied, and returned even nastier than before; they entered her brain and depleted her once lively organs. There was never, "Oh this is stage blah blah cancer" – we never said the "c word" when we saw her. Sometimes, a book selection that our group read referenced someone dying, and it was sad to read, knowing what she might endure.

An uncertain future added to the neck, head, and body pain – by-products of the powerful, wretched chemo and radiation therapies. Her once flouncy thick hair cracked off, then grew back brittle; it no longer shined. The wig we had shopped together for was now also a thing of the past. Some days she appeared disheveled as she shuffled and leaned on the walls or someone's hand for balance.

There was no more yoga for Vanessa, but she was the one who got me into a regular schedule. I used to go sporadically in gyms or on vacation until she finally opened my eyes to Merilynn's wisdom yoga church classes.

All those who loved her, and there were many of us – in the neighborhood, from kindergarten playgroups, a cellist, and members of the book club that had continued for twenty-six years – lovingly witnessed the unimaginable happen. It must have been the hardest on her handsome, kind husband; the perfect gentleman and astute businessman. He watched his beautiful bride break down; he cooked, hit balls on the tennis courts, prepped meals, played piano keys, and occasionally went out for a "rinse" (Vanessa's term for meeting a friend for a drink).

Deeply concerned about her continued pain, we had no choice but to take her doctors' word that she was comfortable. I also prayed that my sweetest friend, an avid reader, would be able to read some of my writings one day. I had gotten some of my emotions out of my head and onto paper in my writers' group.

During her final hours, when Covid had us locked in our homes, writing helped me release from worry and lean into acceptance without attachment to her physical body. I observed her lackluster eyes and knew her end was near. I sat with her, talking aimlessly in her bedroom one late afternoon; I held her feet in my hands on her couch. I learned that no words could adequately describe what it felt like to watch my best friend die.

Keeping her memory, honoring all our loved ones' undying spirit offers us solace and continued connection.

May 15, 2020

> *Dear Friends and Family of Vanessa,*
>
> *On behalf of our dear friend, Vanessa, she passed away last night peacefully in her home, surrounded by love. I write with deep heartfelt condolences.*
>
> *She's in the clouds,*
> *her memory a blessing,*
> *and in some unknown way,*
> *an undying spirit lives on,*
> *that which will never end.*
>
> *Sending each of us extra strength. As the sun went down, Vanessa's body was free and at peace tonight. She now lives on in our hearts and nature with everyone.*

*There is no planned memorial service. We'll reach out
again if there is a way to come together soon to honor our
sweet friend.*

*As requested, please don't send flowers. Instead, and
without obligation, feel free to contribute to Memorial
Sloan Kettering or anywhere you'd like to honor our dear,
beautiful, kind (and sweetest girl I ever met, my soul sister,
book buddy) friend.*

Feel free to forward this email to anyone you'd like to.

With Love,

Marla

As I moved into grief, I knew it was up to the wise woman
in me to endure my emotions. Finely tune and sharpen my
body's heightening fits of lost love. Each soul-to-soul experience can feel like a daunting vision when our best friends or
loved ones who want to live are going to die. Yet there was
no doubt her body was depleted after years of fighting. Her
love remains everlasting.

And so I prayed that my dear friend's soul had been set free
from the toxic stressor that turned into a beastly disease.

May Vanessa's name be a blessing.

Where we find or stumble upon a licensed mental health therapist, yoga teacher, reiki practitioner, retreat or health wellness center encouraging us to release whirling tidal waves in
our minds. Women are influential creators. We can surround
ourselves in healthier communities, be awestruck by nature's

abundance, emote inner joy through effective communication, and foster meaningful relationships and radiance.

The earthly plane offers so much for us to reimagine and discover during our lives, and when the day comes for our loved ones to return, their spatial energy remains, even as dust.

Death and Dying

My grandmother, Nana Ann, left a profound impact on the world. Though her life was filled with turmoil, as her granddaughter, I always felt her love.

Growing up, I overheard hushed stories from aunts and uncles about the aftereffects of their confrontational encounters with her. I observed their opinions, yet my bond with Nana remained unscathed until I visited my grandparents' apartment in Florida one day.

I had a college break and flew south to help my Pop Pop Harry heal after surgery. He had always been diligent with his fitness routine, swam daily, and had a gentle disposition. I was eager to be with them and lend a hand in his recovery.

Nana was used to prepping meals for Pop Pop in their five-by-five-foot, linoleum-floored apartment kitchen.

In it, she sprinkled sugar on strawberries for us kids any time we visited and made perfect Mandelbrot cookies (a Jewish dessert that originated in the early nineteenth century – a close relative to Italian biscotti, first made in the Middle Ages).

On day three, she expressed an opinion that felt like a personal attack on me. This happened in the small hallway beside

Nana's kitchen. At that moment, I was enthusiastically sharing my first-hand experiences of studying abroad in various European countries and learning about our shared humanity and diverse cultures. Nana kept defending her belief that traveling anywhere, especially out of the country, was unnecessary because we could learn about faraway places in books.

Our scuffle deflated my joy and caused a brief division. I failed to see things from her point of view. *Why didn't she understand me?* In retrospect, I realized it wasn't my place or responsibility to alter her opinion.

One day, I recalled Nana and our long-ago incident during a meditation. Another time, I wrote her name during the *Ho'oponopono* process on a card with the words, "I am sorry, please forgive me, thank you, and I love you." I lifted a lingering veil and peered into sadness; I readjusted the story with compassion for the woman she was. Although we were related (my father's mom), we grew up in different times and circumstances. She was my elder, and I appreciated our relationship. I set my hold on her free as my energy was lifted. With her spirit's guidance, I further released any leftover resentment.

Healing a relationship wound takes patience and forgiveness, whether the other person is on this or another plane. Clearing negative energy and bridging pathways toward freedom can strengthen and heal some underlying bonds even after someone dies.

In her book *Remember Love: Words for Tender Times,* poet Cleo Wade eloquently reminds us to welcome togetherness through fragility:

**"When we own our errors,
when we offer apology,
we contribute to the collective oneness."**

Although she had passed away decades earlier, muscle memory tension from our confrontational turmoil lingered in my bones. I felt terrible for trying to prove my point. Revisiting the emotional heat of our unsettled debris fed my psyche with solace. I lovingly renewed my relationship with Nana Ann, freeing myself from disharmony. Saw her through the lens of compassion. I've better understood why people do what they do: many people with unresolved painful emotions inflict pain onto others. Some are born into a family of present and or generational heartache. We were all once innocent children. A baby relies on an adult's love. Our nervous systems and hearts must recover if love is not apparent due to detached relationships.

Recalibrating our world to gain brightness operates on collective power. Speaking up by honoring our physical and mental entities can pave the way for future generations. When a woman partakes in diffusing degradation, she can break free from negative patterns. One individual's conscious decision to self-attune can change their entire family's future trajectory.

The loss of someone due to death or for any reason can prompt feelings of devastation. However, it also sheds light on the importance of living. Grief is an emanation of love. It offers hope for healing relationship wounds, providing a neutral playing field where we no longer battle. Entering a new spiritual zone and connecting with loved ones is a possibility for us to explore.

In the Jewish tradition I grew up with, naming babies after a deceased relative is customary. My Hebrew name, Miriam, honors my maternal grandmother, Marion, as does the initial M in my English name. It means a connection to God, who never saw the bitterness. My cousins Michelle, Melissa, Kelly Melissa, and I were all given our names, for the matriarch we, along with eight other grandchildren, never had the chance to meet. In this way, whether through ceremonial names or informal names, we are reminded to keep their memory alive in our own unique way, either before or after they've departed.

My friend Heather established the Show Me Your Heart Foundation in memory of her son Eugene, who had battled a health crisis on and off for years of his young life. She, an Asian American, has become an inspirational voyager promoting and showcasing emerging and renowned classical musicians and eccentric artist forms. Additionally, her foundation encourages young aspiring adults to assert themselves as leaders and creators and raises funds benefiting multiple children's hospital medical programs.

The IronMatt Foundation was created to honor another young boy's courage (see Appendix). Looking into his wise, knowing eyes, we felt our hearts overflow with exuberance. He left the sweetest, kindest impression, gifting us strength and youthful grace.

Children helping children is an intuitive act of innocent play. Our youngest, Rachel, was in pre-K and kindergarten with Matthew. She and her classmates painted pictures and wrote letters to their beloved friend when he missed school or activities, weakened by treatments and challenged by illness.

Today, the organization provides financial support and comfort to families fighting childhood brain cancer. Matt lived life to the fullest—though brief—reminding us to savor life's simple joys and to spread happiness widely. Some children learn life-long lessons far too young, such as how to say goodbye while keeping a loved one's memory alive.

Yet without the pain and suffering, or the muddy struggles and eventual acceptance, there would be fewer reasons for new chapters of medical breakthroughs, moments of laughter, or lotus petals unfurling to rekindle brightness. These are what help us regain momentum and reignite the sparkles of radiance, purpose, and intentionality once again.

When any form of grief, whether from a physical loss, a relationship breakup, or family dysfunction, holds us hostage, our minds are left to linger. Yet these emotions can be transformed and repurposed.

Sticking together through thick and thin with the ones we love has inspired me to shed light on navigating the unbearable landscapes of loneliness, self-doubt, and fear, and on improving our relationships. Our marriages, like friendships at any age, gain meaningful depth when we adapt to changing times.

Rebuilding a present or past relationship by welcoming signs such as a bird landing nearby or hopeful messages crossing our path, can serve as a therapeutic and healing form of reconciliation, creating a deeper connection if we trust the process.

The Radiant Woman's Way

Since the negative mind chimes in 9 out of 10 times, engaging in something positive helps us to rearrange our thoughts.

Candle-gazing: changing your approach to recognize the indications of affection.

- Stare at a candle or focus on a single point, like a spot on the floor, wall, or out a window.
- Inhale patience.
- Exhale acceptance.
- When a thought comes; watch it go.
- Repeat 1-3 minutes.

Next...

- Close your eyes.
- Visualize a beautiful scene (consider a beloved or an aspect in nature) for an inward gaze.
- If a negative thought arises, replace it with a self-affirming mantra like:

  I am one with the Universe; I am radiant, I am light.

  Repeat 1-3 minutes.

Consider incorporating celestial hand movements for a special touch. Additionally, infuse affection and synchronize vocals with gestures to create a song-like sound.

- Begin rolling your hands at the heart center as you say (or sing), *"I am one with the Universe."*
- Open palms with elbows in toward the ribs and repeat,

"I am radiant, I am light."

Duration: 3-5 minutes.

To customize your experience, create a personalized mantra.

Chapter 13

CONFESSIONS OF
A RADIANT WOMAN

"Life is the flower for which love is the honey."

~Victor Hugo

Uncovering why I turned to others for approval instead of becoming self-reliant, in part, led both to my downfall and entrance into redefining my purpose and role in life.

Questioning why I was born was part of my quest for better health. It allowed me to fail and try another way to uplift myself and better serve others.

If only I had found an answer to my quest sooner, I sometimes asked my older, wiser self, yet my past heartaches funneled me into a rhythmic purpose.

When my health faltered due to constant aches and pains, I was determined to uncover root snags before my body went further awry. My research forced me to investigate alternative solutions that supported my well-being by answering my request to relieve ailments. It gave me new terms and conditions to live my best life.

Each bump and hiccup offered new routes. Instead of quick-fix Band-Aid medications, I chose mantra, music, and meditation.

Every relationship we encounter, from birth to adulthood, influences the days ahead. Many women aspire to be admirable caretakers, partners, friends, colleagues, and business associates as they integrate their lives with others, reshaped through partnerships and marriage. As our relationships shift, we make peace with what is. Our love, integrity and limits are constantly tested. After experiencing years of stress, finding a safe space to share our untold stories can help reprogram our minds by allowing us to open ourselves to acceptance. It deepens our desires to bring connective meaning into our relationships.

Even as I strived to feel better, at my worst, when my body broke down, there were days and weeks that I wanted to die (see Appendix for suicide/mental health resources). Rattled emotions stirred up my addictive behaviors. Under the covers at night riveted by overwhelm. If not for this darkness, I might have never discovered my hidden talent and continued to surf only on the surface waves.

On a family ski trip, each daughter separately said, "Mom, why don't you try to stay more radiant?" I guess I had complained one too many times about my aching knees and shin discomfort from the boot rentals. Although I wanted to shine on the Colorado slopes, it was not easy for me to keep my morale. I knew it was up to me to put my best foot forward in outdoor slope adventures. I loved feeling the wind on my face beneath azure skies during wet-whipped snowy days. When or if that day comes when the rigorous demands of cold sport are not meant for me anymore, then I will convert it to another fresh-air game.

If I embody radiance, those around me will reflect it to me. I am grateful for the ability to examine my patterns, improve my mindset, and prevent negative cycles from repeating. By being conscious of our thoughts and behaviors, we can magnify our brilliance and spread positivity to others.

If we want to be the best version of ourselves in a partnership, expressing our feelings rather than suppressing them can relinquish fear or worry.

Cooped Up in 2020

During the first year of our global pandemic, I treaded on fear of the unknown.

Newsflashes and confinement tested societal weaknesses and strengths. Many, including myself, fell victim at some point to depressive states. The global loss of lives gravely impacted their struggles and losses.

I prayed, meditated, and flowed on my yoga mat to release stress. Pounded my feet on the black hardtop pavement of my neighborhood's streets. Spent time crouched over my computer screen, interacting with social media while crafting personal business goals. Searched for ways to pivot online by offering women stress relieving meditation programs. Each outlet helped to free my mind.

Yet, by that bizarre junction of spring 2020, when seated more than I was accustomed to, my usual on-the-go mode further halted.

Complexities derived from the never-ending news creeping in. So did back pain. It brought me down a slippery slope that I had never known before.

Simultaneously, my dearest friend Vanessa died after her ten-year battle with Lynch Syndrome. To top off the week, though not dire, Jonathan had knee surgery.

He stood up on crutches by himself even though a nurse was there to escort and assist him to my car, where I waited per Covid precautions. She then peered into my window and wished me good luck with a smirk and wink. *Aha,* I thought to myself, *the doer who loves to be in charge and fix everything independently will finally take some time off and rest.*

Meanwhile, in my grief, excruciating pain pierced down my lower back. The discomfort around and inside of me challenged my purpose. *How to soothe others when it pained me to stand or sit?* Flat out on the couch felt best. I could barely wait for bed... yet not before I served our family *Shabbat* (a ritual time to rest, reflect on the past week, observed by many Jewish families) dinner. Plus, our Rabbi would honor my friend's memory on Friday night's service. For years, her name was read aloud weekly on Friday for *Mi Shebeirach* (a "get well soon" healing prayer of body and soul that concludes with *Amen*) at our temple. I rushed to log onto Zoom for the service.

I felt pressured by the time as I placed *Challah* (a sweet Jewish egg bread, shiny and braided), candles, and glasses on the table for the traditional fruit of the vine blessings. Jonathan hobbled to the table and reached for the clicker as I put finishing touches on our meal.

"No TV!" I snapped. It irked me when he surfed channels and watched before or during meals for big games and essential news (aka COVID precautions). His insistence on keeping the news on until we officially sat down to eat threw me over the edge. I reached my boiling point, feeling disrespected and invalidated in my desire for a more peaceful room. Frustrated, I raised my voice and shouted to convey my message.

When misspoken words fly out of our mouths, our radiance dims. I wished my reaction had not taken on his energy. What made matters worse was that I forgot to turn the mic off. Not only had my jarred words hit my family, they projected out to our rabbi, cantor, choir, pianist, and guest musician at the start of the evening congregation service, as well as any members already logged on. I was so embarrassed. My throat hurt the day after as a reminder.

It felt like I had been thrown out into left field, cornered by a mound of physical burns while intense emotions bubbled over and pain traveled down my left leg and foot. I felt myself hit rock bottom again.

Usually, if something in my body felt off balance or my thoughts were skewed, yoga poses and flows, acupuncture, and massages cleared my blocked channels. My hatha yoga flows were less than routine. Those latter options were out of the question since most businesses, including my life, were in lockdown mode.

Yet, knowing I had overcome calamities before where pain in my body led to other health battles, I was determined to beat my frustration, doubt, and discomfort away. At the time, I didn't know I had full-blown sciatica. I avoided steroid shots, though recommended, and sought out exercises and tai chi and virtual sessions online over Zoom with Veronica, an intuitive healer. The book *Back on Track* for fitness and back pain is now available (see Appendix).

The Radiant Woman's wealth of experiences teaches her to recycle pain and rise again.

While my sister Abby nicknamed me *Little Miss Perfect* long ago (and to this day we laugh about it), I've had many shortcomings. I would be remiss if I didn't admit I could have cleared the air before or after speaking words I later regretted. Mistakes are a natural part of life.

Reaching for perfection based on what others think of us can keep us hostage. Covered emotions can block our creativity, intuition, and make us feel inferior.

> ### *It was the moment not just to recuperate,*
> ### *but to flourish.*

One night in the company of women I knew, I felt out of sync. Drank one too many tequilas on a mostly empty stomach. Threw up over the deck of a gorgeous night sky that overlooked the ocean's bay. I was grateful to my friends for getting me home safely and tucked into bed. Embarrassed by my actions, I later uncovered why I felt out of place. My earlier perception noted deception.

We are meant to repel the muck, have a good cry, create masterful pieces, and even get messy to release and detach from people who don't cheer us on. And if we get entangled in the made-up stories in our head, or sense someone else's secret scheme, our bruises over time disappear if we choose to do so. A schemer's decision to clean up their actions is up to the individual. The seeker's purpose remains unscathed when the search enables us to meet ourselves. It also allows us to see right through the person before us.

I'm an open book. I would not, could not, hurt another with intent, nor would I, could I, should I ever intentionally lie because one lie leads to further manipulated stories. Now that that is clear, let's not cover up the fact that there are reasons why some girls/women are mean. Something in their life is unclear. Maybe it stemmed from an insecure moment where they thought covering up their tracks or conforming to societal rules at the cost of not being joyful and free was best, but deception is never a healthy way to thrive.

Why not just tell the truth if we want to have a more intimate party? Not everyone is meant to be our best friend.

Once a woman identifies her honest emotions and moves amid the energy, she can sparkle more.

Conscious refinement develops our superconscious mind. It contributes to causes that give us meaning and purpose because we care to make a difference in the lives of others. In return, we feel better about ourselves by partaking in activities we are passionate about.

We can achieve this by utilizing our meditative mind – wake up 5-10 minutes earlier, or practice anytime during the day or before bed. These arch-lined intuitive tool systems are available to anyone to implement and influence positive energy.

Every human being was born to be of service with intentional purpose. Having everyone agree with us will not make a difference in the end. Elevated beings, spiritual beings driven by their soul's purpose, optimize lifelong learners to flourish.

If any of my children ever received a less-than-perfect grade, I asked if they sought clarifications from their teacher or professor to ensure they learned from their mistakes. Value is not derived from academic achievements alone. Stretching our minds and being tested can help us master subjects we may not have a natural calling for but are required to learn. Striving for perfection and overachievement can become a curse.

When ulterior motives or egotistical behavior gets in our way of being conscious, we lose power.

Repurposing any dark thought by digging ourselves out of rock bottom or messy ditches through mind control can be transformative. Rectifying, recommitting to peace, and turning our eyes on the gentler peace prize leads to liberation.

Listening to Persistent Nudges

When it comes to breaking a habit that is not serving us well, we can change by setting an intention to clean up our actions.

Beginning to observe our instinctual behaviors and asking ourselves questions like, "Why am I reaching for that drink? Is it out of boredom, overwhelm, or worry? What am I truly hungry for?" can help us uncover deeper motivations and needs.

Can we replace the indulgent behavior or thought with new patterns by allowing ourselves to truly see viable options as opportunities for new beginnings?

Investing in yourself might mean choosing ginger water, playing your favorite song and going for a walk, or even doing a silly dance instead of reaching for another sweetened latte or pastry.

Noticing our sedentary habits or emotional patterns in our relationships with others and ourselves can help us uncover why we do the things we do. However, during the process of change, it's important to give ourselves grace – even when we lose the will to choose the healthiest fitness routine or the best meal on the menu.

Why do I still buy sweet caramels at checkout counters, or eat pecan, pumpkin, and apple pie when I wake up after Thanksgiving? Why do I consume alcohol on occasion when I know it is inflammatory?

For when we know that fruit is the kind of sugar our body is designed to digest, we might indulge in that huckleberry pie in Montana (and yes, it was outrageous!). It's okay to give ourselves permission to enjoy a treat now and then, as long as we balance indulgence with accountability, whether that's working with a coach or setting goals and tracking progress with charts.

Coach Kristin of Charis Fitness (see Appendix) advises: "Pick one day for treats and stay more disciplined if you're aiming to fit into a special occasion dress or following a gluten-, sugar-, and caffeine-free diet as recommended – often to combat inflammation or lose weight."

On the days when you fall off the wagon, remember to have compassion for yourself. You can always start again.

Putting things in our bodies or having conversations in our heads that don't serve us or others well are not good to hold onto or digest. Though not easy, it is up to us to be disciplined enough to get back on track.

Am I weak, strong, or human?

From Naked Walls to Empty, Echoey Acoustics

I have a knack for adding a *tchotchke* as a finishing touch for each nook and cranny. Each surface appears neat and spiffy, yet inevitably gathers dust.

When our oldest son drove to Colorado during the pandemic of 2020 and became a full resident a few years later, lots of his clothes and masculine products remained.

Meanwhile, to get rid of stuff, our junk drawers overflowed with rubber bands, lip balms, and pens. Overstuffed closets continued to suffocate me.

I wanted an honest business to help overwhelmed women release stress by creating irresistible offers that conveyed my truth. *How could I when extra baggage (junk drawers) surrounded me?* Getting to the bottom of it felt never-ending.

I gave away twenty beaded bracelets, thirty t-shirts, forty bean-ies, twenty leather clutches, and fifteen pairs of shoes – plus bags of kids' books, Legos, and wooden puzzles (yes, I saved them and had a hard time giving away many prized stuffed animals like froggy).

The Radiant Woman prioritizes organization, hiring an expert if necessary to help her remove clutter because *schmutz* (a Yiddish word derived from German, meaning messiness) can deter her life's progression. She acknowledges how spaciousness feels in external environments as a formula for blossoming in all areas of her home. Each time I tidied up, I felt better.

Doomed or Reliant?

Perfection dominates my character as it relates to my astrological sign, *Virgo*. Navigating through my tendencies by letting go of attachments throughout my life has helped open me up to the surrender passage. All imperfections and struggles are designed to teach us something in the end. Practicing a body scan as a form of meditation can bring us to the moment of quietude as an action-oriented mind process.

Operating from a fullness perspective entertains the happier attraction. Ingrained patterns in our subliminal mind from past events can trigger an entire day to go sour. Shifting from one negative thought to a positive one overcomes the influence of lack, bringing awareness to our minds. We can refashion lack to luster. Recalling a joyful moment from your past can replicate a similar joy and bring more happiness.

The thoughts we go to sleep with go into our dreams. Our state of mind comes along, remembering what we slept with. If we end and begin each day with gratitude, when we swing our feet out of bed, it influences the chemistry in our brains. By focusing on positivity, we can improve our outlook on life.

When worry goes on autopilot, rotate gears. Perpetuate opportunity.

The Radiant Woman reshapes habitual patterns by setting new standards and rethinking her future.

By recognizing nature's shapes and sounds as designs to reshape the space within us, we can transform our doubts. Connecting with literal and figurative sun/moonlight energies can rev our engines, propelling our existence with its eternal light. When we align ourselves with aspects, including tangible and distant elements, we can achieve inner harmony and balance in the imbalance.

Mantras are designed to aid concentration. Their secret code is in the infused vibration.

The primary difference between affirmations and mantras is that they're centered around positive-thinking phrases mainly used to build confidence. In many traditions, a mantra is given to someone who might repeat it for months, years, or even throughout their life. This sacred exchange and discipline can override your consciousness, clearing Samskaras (mental impressions) ingrained in your brain due to your actions, thoughts, and experiences. Over time, these impressions shape our habits and personality traits. Our entire perception and experience of the world can encourage positive or negative effects.

Experimenting with different sound currents and mouth movements, listening, and reciting high pulsations has transformative benefits. Repetitive sounds can calm your subconscious mind even if you do not fully understand an ancient text's meaning.

Making raspberries, like children and adults often do in playful moments, is a quick and easy way to relax your facial muscles.

The act of "flubbering" your lips helps release tension by relaxing the jaw and can even make you smile. Many musicians practice this as warm-ups before singing to loosen up, prepare vocals, and improve performance stamina.

The Radiant Woman's Way

When specific sounds are made from the mouth with a meaningful, healing, and prayerful vibration, it can create a sensation in the crown of the head. Translating a mantra can impart a sense of confidence when repeated by strengthening your mind–body awareness system.

The *"Om"ing* current illuminates light as an offering to navigate obstacles, disappearing within your inner self through sound. Traditional yoga classes in India and sacred temples chant the ancient OM invocation mantra, the Universe's womb sound.[6] It's also known to soothe a newborn baby.

The full AUM syllables involve four levels and symbolic parts of consciousness.

Ahh (past), Uuuu (present), and Mmmmmm (future), to Silence (timeless).

From deep sleep that promotes a dream state, allowing the subconscious to be reprogrammed, to the moment

---

[6] The Mysterious Hindu Om Symbol And Its Meaning | by East Asian Cultures | Medium

you awaken, where dreams can lead to new states of consciousness and auric realm fields.

- To produce the sound, consider closing your eyes.

- Root seat and lengthen your spine.

- Place your hands on each knee in *Jnana* wisdom mudra (thumb to forefinger).

- Chanting the universal sound of "OM" three times or for three minutes is a meditative tool to help you to repair and unwind in real time.

- If you don't want to "chant" (or for kids), you can also receive some benefits by Hummmmmmm-mmmmmming as one might do when something tastes so yummy.

Then, with your eyes still gently closed, take a moment to use sensation to feel your surroundings.

- Scan your body by squeezing and releasing tension from feet to head or head to feet or visualize light going to those places.

- Contemplate and flash-write some afterthought emotions on "how you feel" at the end of the meditation in your tangible or imaginary journal.

Being intentional with your voice, engaging specific muscles from head to toe, brings us into the present moment.

Chapter 14

LOVE, LIGHT, AND STAYING RADIANT DURING THE DARK NIGHTS OF OUR SOULS

Each time you embrace joy in the face of challenge,
you're listening to the internal whispers of your soul.

A few weeks before the pandemic, one of my long-time friends from high school died by suicide. My heart dropped to the ground. I shrieked and cried, "NOOOOOOOOOOOOOOOOOO! Why? How could this have happened?!"

Odd news about a deadly virus outbreak in China and Italy had just started spreading. As those faraway headlines flashed, the tragic news of my friend hit home, shocking my world and those who loved her. It severed relationships with broken hearts. Though Julie lived a few bridges away on Long Island, and we hadn't seen each other in person for years, she remained one of my "BFFs" (Best Friends Forever).

An incredible wife and mom to two beautiful daughters, her life appeared to be going fine, yet her will to live had shut down. As I pondered and mourned her death, I thought:

Why had she, like so many others, lost all hope yet remained silent for the most part?

Suicide is permanent. It does not discriminate on race, gender, or status. If only I had known what she'd been struggling with just a few months earlier when our close-knit friend group had urged her to attend our upcoming big reunion. Maybe she would have revealed her genuine emotions. If only I, we, someone had asked her the right questions before it was too late. If only…

That one month later turned out to be the beginning of her end. *What had her final months of existence looked like and why couldn't her doctors and the few people who knew what was going on make those horrible afflictions to her mind disappear?*

After Julie's first suicide attempt had been hushed, her health and overall mental state diminished further. And in a blink, her joyful presence had gone into a full-fledged altered state of being. Demonic voices, perhaps due to hormonal changes, chemical imbalances in her body, plus mind-altering medications to "*prevent her depressive/suicidal thoughts,*" had clogged her brain further with mistruths and desperation.

And so, I prayed.

I prayed for Julie's undying spirit to live on in our hearts forever. That her family, society, and supportive communities would continue to offer outreach to help families grieve and move on without the person they loved. With all the latest and greatest technological inventions and advances in medicine, we as a human race have so much to learn about the human condition.

I prayed that all beings across the globe would have equal access to healthcare teams who collaborate with medical doctors and therapists by implementing improved awareness and suicide prevention systems.

I prayed that people would be informed of alternative choices when prescribed medication to treat suicidal thoughts. The evaluation process along with collaborative resources remedies needs greater attention. Integrative approaches are paving new frontiers, helping to repattern the patient's nervous system and alleviate tensions and anxieties.

Facing one's true nature by releasing feelings through therapeutics and mindfulness practices can offset the misbelief patterns and break the iceberg of stone-faced human beings. It gives everyone a safe space to breathe and permission to feel while refocusing on what's beautiful in the rubble. There is light at the end of the tunnel. This would halt our beloved friends and family from making an irreversible decision. Resources, compromise and patience are required to prevent history from repeating itself from one generation to another. Transformation and healing from mental illness are possible. *However, why then has society had such trouble eradicating this other pandemic: suicide?*

Why had she, like so many men, women, and teens, lost their will to thrive while others got to the other side of the "disease" (as it's diagnosed here in the States) *inflicted by delusions, drama, and or trauma?* These complex questions are for us to contemplate and speak out on.

As I mourned my treasured friend, I recalled when, as a teen, I learned my father's friend had died by suicide. It frightened me and I cried for the man our family had loved and the family he would never be with again... I remember hearing whispers that his financials had been part of the reason or perhaps the final straw. It's unfathomable to consider someone so distraught that they would even plan for their demise and purchase an insurance policy as security assurance for their loved ones.

Death by suicide is a preventable destination. Mental health instability is staggering. Breaking through barriers of despair is worth the fight. Nothing gets fixed or changed overnight. I have watched people transform on their yoga mats in meditation seats, in group circles. I, like others, have wept, released and shared my secret thoughts. When we keep our emotions inside, they suffocate us. Whether we wear fancy clothes or tattered jeans, no booze, drugs, or insults behind our backs or in the face of others repairs our pain. We must create cohesive allegiance to foundations and advocate for better support systems. It takes a community, a village, a town to get us out of dense matters. We are not meant to dig ourselves out of the messy soil alone (see Appendix for suicide/mental health resources).

The Radiant Woman does not take on what is not hers in terms of feeling like she could have, would have, should have, done better to help their loved ones release from their trauma. Nobody is in control of another being. Listening is one of our greatest assets. Being an advocate for friends and family members' erratic behavior that gets ingrained in their brains needs supportive resources with easier access to holistic mind-body approaches to life.

Mental health challenges affect every family. It lives in every corner of the world, from attached stigmas to reversing the disobedience of our preconditioned monkey minds. Suicide prevention is a global priority and equal citizens' birthright!

If only we were given the tools to calm our anxiety and fears early on in our homes, schools, or places of worship. Managing the comings and goings of our emotions, including our shadow feelings, offers us growth opportunities. When family secrets or shame are carried over from childhood into adulthood, we deplete our energy and fuse. As we age, it is up to us to set ourselves free before bursting out in anger.

It is never too late to begin releasing fears, judgment, and gossip by letting go of our past, removing daily stressors through the present moment, and conscious living.

Professional help and community support exist, but we cannot progress in the demise of our thoughts if we, our clients, family, or friends feel alone. Unresolved behaviors get passed on to the next generation.

Human doers must also rest instead of dwelling in one emotional state. The complex can be broken down as a reminder and call to work towards clearing the root causes of stagnant thoughts. Misinformation not only distorts us, it physically alters our minds. And in the rubble, may each living, breathing, soulful being learn how to reinvent and customize their dream wheel, seeing themselves as the image of love.

Our core high school group bond remained with Debbie, Stacy, Jen, Kacey, and our treasured friend, Julie.

After the loss, our friendships became more vital, drawing us into a closer-knit group ever since the unspeakable lingered over us. We still whisper in soft tones about what went wrong. In the first year, we joined a community walk for suicide prevention. We handled our stress amidst what-ifs by talking openly about our personal lives. Since Julie's unfortunate demise, we've made an unannounced pledge to be open and honest with each other.

If only everyone were given the same open space and permission to say, "I'm not okay today. I'm sad. I'm lonely."

Combating our emotions to move through our temporary states of being can release fear and move us closer to faith.

We trust our intuition to know when to listen and what questions to ask.

Asking, "Is there anything you'd like to talk about?" Turning heavier conversations into small talk and lighter ones into the crux of a serious discussion.

> *Troubled souls, we're sorry for your pain. Although you've lost all hope, we believe in you. The Universe hears your outcry. We pray you'll find another way but if you depart before this irrational mental health state ends, we will pick up the pieces as best we can, remembering you in better times, surrounded by our steadfast love.*

Families and friends are deeply affected by the aftermath of misfortune. If only we could open up and let our loved ones in. The pain can be temporary, even when it feels overwhelming for you or a loved one. Ask for help.

In recent years, there has been growing recognition of mental fragility, including struggles with suicidal ideation and addiction. However, there is still much progress to be made.

This condition demands urgent intervention, possibly involving medication and, most definitely, lifestyle adjustments such as monitoring dietary deficits, food, herbal supplements, doses of nature's bounty, and mindful meditation.

During times of job loss or recession, some families may struggle to afford food. Accumulated challenges in life, such as crossed boundaries, failed crops, illnesses, or situational crises, can lead to one's ability to make clear decisions and lead to a feeling of being trapped.

How do we ease this? Keeping up by saying yes to people and environments that uplift us or no to commitments that might drain us. Slowing down when our bodies and minds require attention before declining to call for help. Building a healthy environment by setting new goals for longevity and endurance. With appropriate interventions and preventive measures, mental discourse can be restored, giving hope for a better future.

People in constant exposure to another day of emergency services, our doctors, nurses, police, volunteers, rescue workers, men and women in service or battlefields, and anyone exposed to trauma on an ongoing basis get startled. They might have flashbacks of the scene triggering their post-traumatic trauma. Their nervous systems might go numb and disassociate from the general population if not tended to.

Suicide walks like the one we went on for our dear friend Julie (see Appendix) bring family and community together to remember our loved ones and bring attention to prevention.

There are no guarantees of tomorrow. We can only control our breath awareness in the "now" of our reactive mind.

The pandemic changed the face of life for everyone who suddenly went eye to eye with the fact that we can never predict or control the unknown. It is inevitable that, just like weather patterns, every relationship vibration reorients even if we have a plan.

Since no one can predict their future, envisioning better days ahead encourages the prospect, despite problems, of resolve in a world where we or our loved ones listen to receive a compliment. Even if it's hard, we acknowledge the pain and commit to getting through by learning how to trust support systems and take wider surveys of our life to see a bigger picture in the universe's glimmers of hope. And by becoming more patient with potential reset offerings and healing processes like practicing mini-moment breath awareness techniques to unmask our personality impulses, we might be able to welcome newfound freedom and avoid dangerous temptations.

If only our friends and families chose to feel what is real – releasing buried secrets and generational fears, buffering over misspoken words to calm past storms, shedding their tears, taking responsibility in the aftermath, rehabilitating settled dust, and transforming relationships into something new.

Nature is equipped to answer our prayers and heal our souls.

Taking our mood temperature is essential since we can only control ourselves.

Seasons change and so do you. As with every ebbing flow, noticing how your thoughts and emotions come and go is the first step in becoming your own thermostat. Tending to yourself before reacting gives us permission to feel a rising or falling sensation.

Becoming a mood barometer allows us to weather our imaginative and real-life storms with alternate routes. In winter, though daylight is shorter and, in many regions, colder, offsetting imbalances before and while inherent change arrives sets us up for emotional empowerment.

For many, the winter blues, also known as Seasonal Affective Disorder (SAD), disrupts daily functions where getting out of bed feels strenuous. The good news is once you identify a pattern, you can become resourceful and take precautions.

When our mood feels dark, depressed or cold, catching our thoughts and making shifts by counting to three before calling, shouting, going numb or letting fuel escalate, can help us put out fiery thoughts, allowing us to self-regulate. Changing our environment or surrounding keeps us on our toes, aware and prepared. Finding a contented middle ground throughout the day can create a steady home base – a place to return to again and again.

Mood regulation involves replacing a negative with a positive. By shifting our perspective, we can embrace this natural cycle, much like hibernating bears, as a time to rest, nest, and reset. It's an opportunity for quiet moments – reading, learning, reflecting, or dreaming of an island getaway by the warmth of a fire.

And if gloom sets in, small adjustments can help. Try listing activities for the warmer months ahead or mapping out plans to ease life's wobbly moments. Even in darker seasons, planning can create light and balance. All withering states are temporary; the sunnyside will rise again.

The Radiant Woman's Way

Changing gears by reimagining your flame.

Take a deep breath and immerse yourself in nature's grace.

Sweat it out with a steamy workout, or infrared sauna.

Cool off with mint tea or a refreshing rose spray mist.

Turn on your internal temperature gauge:

- Walk barefoot to feel grounded and centered.
- Stay playful by sticking out your tongue to catch a raindrop or snowflake.
- Be still and listen to the sounds in nature.

Are you feeling cold from the weather or chilling conversation?

- Wear a sweater and earmuffs, drink hot cocoa, or hug yourself.

- March in place, lifting your knees up.
- Continue marching; tap right hand to left knee, left knee to right for an invigorated glow.

(See the Kapalabhati Breath of Fire as mentioned in Chapter 6.)

Is it hot outside, or are you overheated from hot flashes or a thought?

- Remove a clothing layer.
- Drink H2O to rehydrate.
- Immerse yourself in water or take a cold shower.

Sitali **breathing** ("the cooling breath"). As the name suggests, this chills the body, calming the nervous system. In Ayurveda, *Sitali* breath is encouraged during the summer months and hottest parts of the day to alleviate the heat that builds up in the body.

- Inhale through an O shaped (curled tongue if you have that ability) mouth like you are sipping an imaginary straw.
- Exhale through your nose.
- Repeat.

No one routine has all the answers, but you can command your presence with breath control.

Chapter 15

BECOMING A MOOD BAROMETER BY FORECASTING OUR INTERNAL TEMPERATURE AND TRUSTING OUR INTUITION

"I get up, I walk, I fall down. Meanwhile, I keep dancing."

~ Rabbi Hillel

Though brief, I have experienced episodes when, upon awakening, my body felt depressed. The onset started with either a physical or emotional trigger. I did not want to get up and face the day though knew what was expected of me.

As a young teen, the sudden loss of my Pop Pop Irv had me bursting into tears at random. We sat *Shiva* (as show of respect when a Jewish relative dies). For a week, visitors came with their condolences and support for the mourning. It was strange to spend days with all my cousins after his funeral and sometimes laugh, forgetting why we were there. I was overwhelmed with despair but grateful for the memories of my grandfather being present at my *Bat Mitzvah*, which is a Jewish custom that signifies a child's transition into adulthood at the age of thirteen. That was the last time I saw him. Readjusting to life as it was, I moved on. As a young adult, I felt despondent after a boyfriend's breakup yet better after kicking my legs on my bed while crying into my pillow and talking with friends. Releasing from the emptiness to move through it made room for future relations. In my twenties, spasms triggered piercing aches in my trapezius, neck, and shoulders (perhaps increased by overthinking or maybe that was from the original tickborne infection). My mental state was affected, as were the years of exhaustion and confusion in motherhood. By my thirties, while juggling life as an active mom, wife, and friend – cooking, serving, and kickboxing – I developed patellofemoral syndrome, a condition causing pain in the front of the knee and around the kneecap. When my body lacked physical ease, I persevered to find solutions with each bit of wear and tear.

In my early forties, as each of my youngins grew, I became grateful for those low days that happened while raising kids. The overload gave me a reason to consciously take responsibility for my emotions by using my body and accessing support like I did when growing up. It brought me to a therapist and consistent, conscious yoga practice.

When health mysteries were too much to bear, I welcomed Eastern and Western systems to revitalize my body and soulful spirit.

With each specific hand gesture (like heart mudra, folding my four fingers down and connecting each hand at the knuckles with thumbs facing down and touching together) and mantra-infused meditation, I reprogrammed my mind to believe in myself.

Many ingrained behavior patterns handed down to me from past generations and those I took on in my youth were rebooted.

Learning to adjust invisible thoughts behind closed doors by focusing on what sparked the radiance in me while nobody was watching enabled me to rediscover the real me.

When joining mostly female circle groups online and in-person with all-aged seekers, I noticed that many showed up with at least one foot in, ready to unleash some form of their dormant energy. Collectively, we trusted the transformational process.

Doing whatever it took with the intent to find internal peace, even if it might have appeared to others as being selfish, was and is one hundred percent okay.

As a young adult, I ran a support group through the National Vitiligo Foundation. Those in attendance came with a broad age span of shared stories concerning our autoimmune dis-order, which manifests randomly as white patched skin. I felt extremely uncomfortable, yet proud because I'd orga-nized this chapter. We informed each other of developing treatments, some regulated and others where one traveled to another country for a cream that I too started to use. We released our queries. We discussed "the onset of stress" – some got it older and others younger. There was a death of a loved one, a significant life change.

At one meeting an older woman said people always compli-mented her on her translucent skin tone. I couldn't imagine hearing those words when I was distraught over the loss of my pigmentation. However, as I've aged, I have also encoun-tered the same, "Your skin complexion is beautiful" comment, which has been comforting. Although I have resolved many concerns regarding beauty standards that once bothered me, others persist. The sun I avoided for years has health benefits that I missed out on. Since I burn easily and am less protected from harmful rays without pigmentation, I am prone to other repercussions, including the autoimmune link.

I still get tripped up by where I fit in, whether someone likes me or not, low self-esteem, and outer beauty perfection syndrome. Some of this stems from cover-girl misperceptions. Repatterning illusions by diffusing self-serving egos reveals true radiance.

I appreciated the inclusivity when Barbie® launched a fash-ionista line for petite and other-sized bodies. One in 2020 even had splotched areas on her face, hands, and neck. As a teen-age dermatology patient at Yale Medical Center, I observed others with black or brown skin. I have always felt compas-sion for those with starker tonalities because their contrast was more prevalent. Bleaching is one of the ways to get your skin lighter even quicker. When I was in Russia, I remember seeing a man with vitiligo. It has become more prevalent over the years. Models for *Lululemon* (athleisure) and other brands now have marketing campaigns with vitiligo and other health conditions to invite inclusiveness. From a young age, I learned to have deep compassion for all beings and the cards I had been dealt.

The skin is the largest organ of our body. It is responsible for protection, absorption, and elimination. Applying mild pressure to our skin with a nutrient-rich oil has many benefits, from strengthening the skin's barrier to activating the body's lymphatic draining system to regulating sleep patterns.

I distinctly remember what Melanie shared one day soon after we began meeting, as I have carried my interpretation of her words with me throughout the years: "We all fit into an umbrella of mental states." It depends on what we feed ourselves and what our earlier developmental years instilled in us to believe, or not, that determines our future mental stability and outcome.

Change is inevitable. It has been like this since the beginning of time.

Many years ago, my friend Ilene shared her rendition of a teachable thought that has stuck with me: "If mental health challenges are buried, never adequately healed, or continue to escalate, the mental health illness will perpetuate and worsen as one gets older."

Just like we can train animals to jump through hoops of fire, we can train ourselves to do extraordinary things. We can leave our comfort zones to meet the powerful women looking back at us in our mirrors.

Reforming our thoughts offers us a clean slate perspective. Visualizing snowcapped mountains, arctic glaciers, deserted deserts, the sun and moon rising from coast to coast, splashing waves, calm lakes, starfish, lotus flowers, jungles, forest ranges, or an eagle soaring can help us use our imagination to reinvent and rebuild ourselves.

And in living our ever-changing dreams, we always have a choice to treat each day anew. We can celebrate our accomplishments rather than getting caught in our tracks like deer in headlights.

Life Is a Practice

In the weeks after being told there was nothing to do about my unusual neurological stimuli, I felt hopeless and drained. Once being diagnosed with late-stage Lyme disease, I started regimens to detox through the implementation of Western and Eastern modalities. As my lethargic bouts and discomforted joints persisted, I was determined to resolve the inflammation, which I now know to be my personal life's work – implementing procedures, soaking in Epsom salt baths, reclining on acupuncture tables, sweating it out in infrared saunas (see Appendix for a book on the benefits of sweating), dipping into a freezing cryotherapy tank to relieve joints, pressurized sinus headaches, and stress.

When horrific sciatica erupted, I felt so discouraged again, and, with no relief due to the lockdown, I secretly wanted to die.

In the face of worry, plus myriad physical health ailments, each of my children has also experienced either allergic, auto-immune reactive rashes, intense unexplained joint pain, or other health challenges. At times, I took on their pain when I forgot to release my worry through my meditation toolbox.

Medical mysteries have consumed my beautiful, creative sister's entire adult life. Many doctors ignored her initial inquiries or dismissed her symptoms all together. There's even a term for her unexplained conditions and medical challenges known as *zebra*. At times, her struggles have seeped into my state of being. I still call my sis "Little Red Monkey" for her curious nature and strawberry blond to red auburn hair. We have so many similarities when we chat. Most recently, she spotted a wasp in her apartment as I sat on a lounge chair in my backyard, and one landed next to me.

Life is not always as it appears. Each year I pray my sister's health gets better.

She and I share a few of the same autoimmune disorders, yet my mental and physical health challenges don't compare to hers.

When she suffers, be it from depression or physical ailments, I feel her pain but don't know how to guide her.

Imagine that?

Abby, by nature, is one of the most delightful, playful, and spirited people I know.

A funny girl, she has braved standup comedy (after years of improv) to shed some of her life's complications. In a recent skit with newbie comedians, some were hysterical, and she was one of them.

A dog lover, she was a fantastic pet mom to Juno, who recently crossed over the Rainbow Bridge. I appreciate her affectionate care of our family dog, Mini, when we travel.

After the birth of my first child, she was there for me, offering support and attentiveness during each of my four pregnancies and after-delivery experiences. She entertained the babies as they grew, singing silly songs and sharing playful "Dear Aunt Abby Jill" jokes, like Simon says "touch your toes, touch your nose."

Our sisterly love bond is strong.

She is witty, clever, and brilliant. Both of us are creative women; she colors incredible doodle art and knits original designs, one recent one being our incredible matching ponchos. Together, we belt out classic show tunes and nostalgic jingles like "Wrigley's Doublemint Gum" and "Charms Blow Pop," before commercials changed lanes to being mostly fortified with biological medications.

On some days, Abby's heart is full of love. Yet through the years, her mind is tangled with doubt and mistrust.

When my heart races from the weight of her depressive words – or worse, she says she wants to die – I'm overcome with fear. I fear for her life and the thought of mine without her in it.

Though I attempt to be gentle, if she disagrees and our misunderstandings escalate, the heaviness lingers. My resolve often crumbles when one reply leads to another, and we're caught in a spiral. I believe in her and am proud of how she tries to adopt new behaviors.

In moments I feel unhinged, I amp up my radiance method toolset. Yoga, meditation, less social media, more Reiki, writing, creative outlets, and appointments with healers. I also protect my energy by safeguarding my electromagnetic field with mantra, movement, and music.

Abby is wholesome, pure, and perfect. She is magnificent, and I hope she someday recognizes that self-soothing is the key to honoring her radiance.

Are the prescribed medications many of us take for focus, sleep, depression, discomfort and so on, masking our true emotions or ability to discern realities?

When we take on the energy of another person's
drama and trauma, we too suffer.

In conjunction with sending love out to others, self-exploration resets our minds, guiding us to see ourselves.

When we refrain from repeating any health defining statement, we readjust the projection of our physical image.

We become our forklift by doing the opposite of worry/anxiety. Facing our fears of the unknown, surrendering to what is going on to keep harmony and peace percolating.

When we dismiss depressive thoughts by sitting quietly in nature, on a bench, in a cozy corner of our home, we create a zen space. These simple exercises allow us to carve out new neurotransmitters that increase our will and another person's destiny to receive. It is in this way our love becomes a radiance prayer.

Grief is Real

Sharing memorable stories by speaking our loved ones' names aloud keeps their spirits alive. In Judaism, we say, "May his/her memory be a blessing." My niece and her husband lost their firstborn, Jacob, after thirty-nine days in the NICU (Neonatal Intensive Care Unit). In her learned grief, she shared the importance of saying her baby boy's name out loud. Some ignore or resist speaking a loved one's name, thinking it might provoke upset in those grieving. The aftermath of avoidance brings pain. Grief lasts…

It is up to the living to uplift each other's spirits by connecting through memories of the deceased.

Suppressed emotions in any form are debilitating.

Keeping our loved ones' undying spirits alive moves energy fields.

Both death and physical health scares are actual touchpoint tests of life. Mysterious uncertainty exists in our world at large.

It is important to unwrap our grief, expose our tender emotions, and represent our loved ones in their absence while we live.

When two separate families in our community lost their young sons from pediatric brain tumors, two courageous women on different paths dedicated a portion of their lives to helping others through separate foundations. Some have lost their children to the drug epidemic, like dear Catie who left behind her twin sister. I have observed many of these mothers; women give back and get up again even after the darkest nights of their souls. *The Radiant Woman Shines* is my way of giving back in times of heartache. Death never has good timing, yet living knowing we never know how we might help another deal with a tragedy is a display of humanity.

When our beloved uncle, a sport-loving man, was hit by a truck while riding his bicycle, we were all shaken up. A friend's daughter, Montana, young, bright, and full of light, collapsed one night and never woke up. Inexplicable accidents, unexpected traumas, and sudden deaths. How do those of us left behind manage to live on? Even when you know someone is sick – like my relative who battled addiction for many years and, eventually, died from pancreatic cancer. Losing a loved one hurts deeply. It's painful to know we'll never see or hear their voices again.

Changing the trajectory of our raging weather storms on any day extends random acts of kindness for ourselves to others.

Navigating Our Emotional Rollercoaster Ride

In my extensive research to uncover the meaning of life, I dug deeper into my roots. Widened my inquiry parameters through movement, breath awareness, and conscious conversations.

As a yoga and meditation mentor, I share the same basic formulas that still influence my determination to leave a legacy for my family and a soft imprint on planet Earth. Changing our views opens us to passions. When we tap into our simmering desires, we unlock dormancy.

I wholeheartedly believe that what has brewed unequivocally inside me, in its unique way, lives inside you too.

Sometimes we lose sight before adjusting the knobs of our internal thermostats. Even if we have a support system with practiced tools in place, implementing them in real time to get ourselves out of depressed states faster takes patience. Most autoimmune conditions, mental states, and or dis-eases are rooted in infectious stress. Why fret when love, self-awareness and self-worth can reverse the discord? Elevating our consciousness is a choice, as is rejuvenating mobile stamina, investigating to discover, meditating to create, and befriending ourselves, we ultimately swim through our river's current flow, even when a personal or global crisis arises.

Trusting Our Intuition

When patients and doctors alike ask good questions, listen, and search for answers (beyond what is written in textbooks), their hands-on, personal adaptations adjust to influence their decisions. Similar to the relationship between a student and teacher, if you're looking to boost your intuition, consider the practice of attunement.

Reflective moments are crucial for healing our mind, body and soul.

Doctoring is not absolute. It is a medical "practice" that fosters precision for surgical and or specific procedures. It also gives us muscles to be our own health and wellness advocate.

Books, computers, and technology can never replace the intuitive knowledge within us. Human eye contact speaks volumes, connecting us in ways that technology cannot. When our third eye – our intuition – opens, we align with the universe and tap into life's bountiful abundance.

Getting back on the train by reinforcing the belief that anything's possible, and playing full out by setting our phones aside often changes our internal landscape. When we act daily to trust that it is up to us to express our emotions and use any depressive state as fuel to signal us to do what it takes to get out of it before it takes over, we're in our cosmic driver's seat. In addition to self-reliance, we can partner with others. Seeking help from external sources such as medical professionals, grief support teams, counselors, meditation mentors, trained specialists, health and wellness trainers, or intuitive coaches can provide the support we need.

We can capture a beautiful moment by changing our environment or picturing a new scene or destination. Explore the art of scribing to release outdated stories and trade them with fresh, positive perspectives. Breathing in the opportunity allows us to use our internal and external voices to strengthen us.

It is okay to feel empty and open at the same time. Use the discomfort as fuel and remember that the sun will shine again. Solar, lunar, and the all-mighty spirit surround and are within us and live on even as dust settles and the physical body is no longer visible or present in our lives. All emotions from our past relationships, from yesterday or decades ago, can revisit us and rise on any day of the week. Rare gems might appear in the cloud formations, bird flaps, and surging storms. With patience and time on our side, just like the newborn cries, we too can shake off the stress, wiggle and squirm our way through the rubble as a formula to release burdens of yesterday by tuning into the presence of now. Look ahead by processing physical pain and loss of any relationship breakup by separating our ego from the ultimate truth and love. Notice our brothers, sisters, friends, foes, and neighbors as majestic. Each of us ripens in our way, from dark wombs to wounds of wonder with no guarantee of tomorrow.

Accessing Your Muse's Potency

Imagine diffusing an anger chip on your shoulder by checking your inner peace thermometer. Initiating magnification toward something peaceful or beautiful. Moving into acceptance of what is (our breath and reaction) instead of anticipating what's not in our control.

It's not if but when, as we attempt to figure life out while facing an obstacle, we use a specific slowed-down or quickened breath at any time of day. We could deflate feeling depleted or defeated.

Take time to wander on a spiritual path to grow luminosity, feel for yourself as you do for others by breathing to create harmony and contentment in the lasting partnership with yourself.

When I finally talked out loud, voiced the confused thoughts in my head with Melanie and practiced quietude, I got unstuck. As I pointed my heart's arrow in another direction and reshaped my reactive mind to unknown outcomes, I felt and tasted the salty-sweet bitterness of emotions moving through me. I no longer felt afraid to try something new for myself, like when I opened *Naturally Yoga's* double-door entrance with its temporarily held police station. If I had never walked in and stayed with my old self, I would not have found my new road map. Fear would have gotten its way.

A yogi begins his or her struggle in the womb. From their limber, movable joints and kicking legs, they are born with survival instincts that depend on early guidance and support. As we age from childhood into adulthood, the comparison game inhibits our higher state of relationship growth.

You don't have to bend like a mint green *Gumby-like* character to practice yoga. Meditation is for anyone, yet only some are eager to slow down their thoughts and uncover shadows.

If we all stopped to take a breather, life might get easier. It sets us free and helps us move to lightheartedness instead of attachment to perplexing conversations.

Once we endure struggles from a bird's eye observer perspective, we too can begin to make shifts to find more joy in both simple and complex moments.

Some rules and games, like "Don't step on the sidewalk cracks," were meant to be broken. Our youthful selves remind us to giggle like kids – it's good for the soul. In any informal setting, laughter can serve as a meditative solution. A simple "ha, ha, ha" or "ho, ho, ho" encourages playfulness and reminds us to lighten up!

There's no better time than now to invite our inner teacher to appear. Begin by looking out for tiny miracles throughout your day to shift your entire state of being in this lifetime rather than going on autopilot or for quick-fix coverups. Deep dive expression might get messy at times, though it can also give us a prescription for radiant living. It offers guidance to shed our old skin and clear the cloudy matters of the mind. Stimulating joy in return gives us reason to trust our reflections as exemplary stars in the Universe.

Many cultures and countries are flexible with their time. Some take siestas, longer lunches and explore new paths to experience joy in the here and now. When I visited Jeremy the year he traveled abroad in Barcelona, he leaned his elbows on the table while we dined – and let me know that it was considered impolite to do otherwise. He said to lean in when conversing as a show of interest or engagement. Some etiquette rules are meant to be broken to bring us closer to the ones we love. As a courtesy, perhaps reserve properness for moments like tea with the Queen or showing respect to women and men of service, offering our undivided attention and quietude when appropriate. At other times, we can embrace fun with outlandish applause, making joyful splashes in a water's way.

When we sit on a park bench a little longer, linger in nature, take a walk with a friend, fit in relationship connections, and let go of our to-do list, radiance thrives. These delightful decoys are designed to manage the dire aspects of our minds.

Many women, men, parents, and children have waited on the sidelines of their potential – hopeful yet living in the shadows of their pasts and vicariously through their children, coaches, role models, movie/athletic stars, teachers, professors, bosses, and influencers instead of cultivating a relationship with themselves. Prioritizing our health and wellness to develop with powerful body and mind energy like our children's is necessary for physical strength and growth.

We evolve by surrounding ourselves with people from whom we can learn, making good use of our time. As technology thrives on innovation and advanced speed, slowing down as the yogis and mystics did long ago adjusts our lives. We bypass identifying with commercialized byproduct entities and instead walk on courageous, noble paths of righteousness before moving toward or away from what we're attracted to or uncomfortable with. Our learned experiences help us decipher differences in our tastes between likes and dislikes, each leading us to become shinier.

Human species, presented with ever-changing natural gifts throughout their "life's ambitions," wear their signature smile/brand. When we learn or are intuitively drawn to doing something we love, our "work is never work," as my dad says. People turn to us for our experiential knowhow. What we are attracted to learn often becomes a skill we acquire and can share with familiar ease.

As we bring favored pastimes, passions, talents, or hobbies into our future, some are meant to be set aside so we can enter new territory and reinvent our love interests. This means the continuum of repurposed fuel has no end. First impressions can sprinkle like fairy dust sparks long after our bodies leave Earth. By choosing to spread beams of radiance, we weave together strings of precious memories that will last for ions.

There is a beautiful Hebrew phrase, *l'dor va'dor,* which means "from generation to generation."

Continuity of traditions and values passed down through families strengthens connections. If we learn something sacred and pass it on, we become the sage, bonding families and people together throughout the ages. Passing the Torah scroll from grandparents to parents and then to their children, who read from it during their Bar/Bat Mitzvah ceremony, is one of those significant traditions. I treasure this moment for each of my children on their monumental day.

When it comes to raising responsible children, we hope to instill in them the ability to make themselves, their parents, and educators proud – not just through their achievements, but through their character. Encouragement is key.

Following to stay in a straight militant line when life is curvy can have us reaching for someone else's dreams instead of ours. We can acknowledge our accomplishments when we reverse-engineer to fulfill our desires, not others. Promoting ultimate buoyancy.

Then we go after shiny objects and temptations; if we have developed morals, we are led down one path. We can question and expand our perspective if we follow a religion or someone. If a dent remains, our tarnished relationships are displayed for our children to mimic. It's up to the clergy, parents, teachers, elders and heroes to lead by example for younger generations. Critical thinking instead of following by rote creates change. Honoring our elders by respecting aging beliefs and religious differences opens us to human rights. Heartfelt conversations with intention, instead of passing down discriminating (see swastika blog on antisemitism - Glossary) poker chips, provide us with the fortitude to weave our energies and the great tapestry of life together.

For if a motif that once represented good fortune could take on new meaning due to ignorant propaganda and mistruth, then it is up to the minority voice to remain calm and neutral for the descendants of Hebrew slaves to avoid dysfunction, preventing a repeat of history, while praying reverently for honest hope. As a Jewish American, throughout my life, I have felt the brunt of being a minority. Yet, it has also given me sensitivity and curiosity about who I am and how to learn to respect other cultural and religious practices. With all due respect for others' beliefs, we can learn to love, cherish, and respect each other if we choose to love, not hate.

Being a grown up requires discernment and responsibility. It means you treat others the way you would want to be treated. We treat our husbands, wives, partners, children, parents, elders, farmers, construction workers, spiritual leaders, doctors, flight and bathroom attendants, sweepers, and park keepers as our next of kin. We never know when our actions might uplift another or stop someone from harming themselves or another. Our presence matters. Our hearts beat, pulsing to connect us. Politics, religious views, and many policies divide. It's time for women to take pride in all phases and release from comparison by refraining from gossip. To help reshape the men and fathers of our world into a conscious kind, accept people for who they are, and take care of our self-worth so we don't crumble – bringing beautiful impressionistic rituals into our family to pass on radiance teachings to future generations.

Legacy's influence relies on our holiest selves to prioritize love as the goal.

I remember my sister-in-law telling her kids she had eyes behind her head. She found a way to see my niece and nephew in her microwave's reflection, and from that, her kids took their place. She was playful even when disciplined, and though her approach differed from mine, I respected her mysterious wit.

We get unstuck by regaining our powerful presence and taking ownership of our future - turning each page of life into a playground.

The Radiant Woman's Way

Thank yourself for coming along on the ride with me thus far...There's still more to come, so don't leave just yet.

I used to think that being a great woman meant taking care of you before me. Then I found a new way.

Tree love

- Sit under, near, and walk among the trees.
- Hug a lean one or a wider trunk.
- Notice the differences.
- Place your hands on the bark.
- Use a magnifier to zoom in on the mysterious overlay.
- Place both hands on a solid-sized tree trunk.
- Walk hips and legs back for a downward dog stretch variation.

When we change the narrative by becoming a spectator instead of an actor, and add humor and adventure into our days, it frees our minds to watch our life like it's a movie. By stepping back before reacting, we become a witness to our consciousness.

CONTEMPLATIVE CONCLUSION: A BIRD'S EYE VIEW

"If you want to fly, you have to give up everything that weighs you down."

~ Toni Morrison

After losing touch with a close friend due to my one-sided opinion via email, I realized in making my case that I had not considered what it would feel like to be the receiver. I thought it read clearly, which felt important to me. I might never have pressed send if I had waited to settle some of my emotions, consulted with my husband or an outside source, or listened to my otherwise intuitive mind. Did you know we can sometimes write letters to release stressors without ever sending them because our reactions are often wrapped up by insecurities no other person will solve? However, this was before I developed a keener sense; the repercussion of my careless action was a severed friendship. Reflecting on my part, I realized it "took two to tango." Certain relationships need breaks from one another. Others are not meant for repair, yet living without resolution causes unfinished business to linger.

Many years later, I sent a handwritten letter to apologize. I wanted to clear the path to move forward, but our friendship still needed time to heal. Even when one partnership has physically departed and another is not yet ready to be mended together, we can still write letters to prevent our cynical minds from overreacting or reenacting negative charges.

During another forgiveness program with Shubhraji (see Appendix), she shared various techniques for shifting energy away from our heavy-hearted situations. She suggested writing someone's name related to a confrontation on a card to offer acceptance and forgiveness, which resonated with me. She then guided us to stand up, close our eyes, and visualize the person. We raised one hand high and made a sweeping motion across our torso as if using an invisible sword to sever the aspect of a relationship binding us. This is known as cutting the cords.

Again, the renowned Vedanta teacher from India steeped in meditation, offered us the *Ho'oponopono* approach (discussed in Chapter 3).

If you too want to spark energy to update a current or past relationship, write down what you want to resolve in that relationship(s).

Sense what it would feel like to reconnect energetically with neutrality. This could help ease tension, resolve and improve relations, whether you meet again one day in person or simply think of them.

Breathe through the nose with an audible exhale from the mouth to clear congestion. We can reshape the currency of our relationships with patience and love even if the past friction resulted from an unfair situation. We can reacquaint ourselves with energetic or tangible healing. Clearing negativity for ourselves, regardless of what the other party does, reshapes our future.

Now, through your grand vision, see the relationship as resolved.

Shifts take time, and it took over a decade for that friend and me. Personal growth can restore faith when faced with obstacles, drama, trauma, fear, or unresolved matters. It allows us to let down our guard and rediscover tenderness within ourselves and our relationships. Many are led to therapy, yoga, meditation, nature and other health and wellness modalities to cope with stress. A new lens on life's fragility can rekindle a dwindling flame.

And that's what happened. The Universe hears our calls. Some friendships pick up as if you last spoke yesterday. Move into ease, acceptance and deeper connection. In our situation, we made a natural comeback; other relationships are meant to be set free forever. We can still move forward in our lives, even if no future or amends are in sight.

Shortly after we reunited, I found her name along with a few others on an index card tucked in a journal. It was from a forgiveness workshop class where I applied the *Ho'oponopono* exercise. A year later, as our friendship fell naturally in sync, an even older journal excerpt surfaced while I was organizing, revealing the same friend's name, to which I had applied the principle noting my grief at her loss.

Why do many women (including myself), men, and children take the bait that feeds into comparison, judgment, and gossip? Its aftermath can lead to a trapped path.

If only our hearts could speak, and our hands could touch the sky, redirecting us to wander through mossy crevices. We would choose our words wisely, aware of their impact because the backlash affects our legacy and environment. We would shimmy away from hurtful words by consciously speaking words lovingly when applicable and clearly before we press send because we can't take them back.

And perhaps, over time, self-reflection would become our second nature. Relationships would dance with sprite interplay.

Every human experience offers us spiritual beingness. Our brains can reboot the inner depths of our cells and mind. We can alter the destination of our lives.

Oceanic rhythms adjust our lives' ebb and flow currents when we communicate using all aspects of our being, speaking from our hearts rather than our heads.

Delving into our purpose, wanting to feel better by making a difference in the world while feeling accomplished by taking care of our internal and external conversations.

What if we embrace a life of opportunity, free from conflicts?

To some, my yogic lifestyle appeared weird and woo-woo. And for all those friends and onlookers who chose another way, I'm okay and know you are too. I love and accept you as you are.

The Radiant Woman befriends her "frenemies" (including herself) by lessening the brunt of misspoken words or actions.

Every encounter we've made until now will carry over and continue to shape our lives.

Looking out for one another.

Seeking out fixtures that regulate our mood through the gateway of love.

Celebrating our humanness.

Can you see what I see, taste, hear, touch and feel through the earth, water, fire, air and ethereal elemental senses?

It's our right to interpret, project, and reimagine a beautiful scene where the butterfly represents our diverging attention. We would steer away from criticism, cynicism, and judgment and into metaphysical (invisible changes) and intuitive (premonition and a knowing before something occurs) vision.

We're all born with the ultimate power to amplify radiance, and it is meant to be shared for the collective human and cosmic experience.

Radiance can be developed by believing in yourself without diminishing others' shine, a flexible tendon meant to test and stretch our imagination where there are no limits.

In terms of the fashion world, I love wearing makeup and find it meditative when applying concealer, foundation, blush, mascara, and bronzers. Highlighting our features has advantages, as do red nails and lips if you want to make a statement.

Glamour and shopping days alone or with friends and family can be fun. After endless days of pandemic sweats, I appreciate getting dressed up. Sometimes, I'm not in the mood, yet once I go out I'm happy to have taken the time to prim and pamper myself, whether I get my hair blown out or curl it myself. Getting a massage makes me feel great as does a cozy or productive day of fitness and erranding and doing my craft in athleisure. However, I believe in defining your style and even hiring a stylist to help you recycle what you own, discard what you don't need, and select affordable items that build a style with confidence. Cultivate a personal style that's less about the brand or cloth and more about wearing your story. I'm fortunate to have wonderful role models and know honest stylists (see Appendix) who help others feel comfortable in their size by wearing appropriate, timeless clothing and enhancing their features to build confidence through color and trends.

After my first yoga class at the groovy, new-age spa in the woods, I got a few answers about human nature. Years later, my unexpected, contemplative, self-reflection journey restored my past with dignity and propelled me to live in the grandeur of now. My continued search led me to discover the healer within. A meditative mind that promotes intuitive calm permits us to move through life with abundant happenstance. It gives us reason to nurture love by instilling new beliefs as we age.

During the years, I practiced and became a certified instructor at Naturally Yoga, my beloved "home-base" studio; I offered Karma yoga, also known as *seva,* in various ways as a token of gratitude for the practice. I served tea to my teachers, took home bathroom towels and blankets to wash and roll them, and assisted in their classes by checking students in, welcoming new ones, and providing hands-on adjustments while another teacher was teaching. I was able to reciprocate in a studio space that improved my well-being. I'd walk the heel of my hands up on both sides of a student's spine, give her a little shoulder massage when folded over in child pose or stretch another's arms higher in a triangle, grounding feet with hands on hips, offer balance and extension in high lunge or half-moon pose; I moved gracefully and quietly between mats with no specific order. One day, in a class of around fifty students, I noticed that three VIPs – Melanie, Dr. Gail, and Dr. Annalisa (who had also attended yoga training and classes at Naturally Yoga for a brief period) – were there while I was weaving through.

Being a part of the yoga world has allowed me to connect with people from various backgrounds, many searching for inner and outer mind-body strength and peace. They are doctors and clergy, karate masters and masseuses, healers and food servers, business owners, contractors, realtors, postal workers, families, students, children with autism, therapists, veterinarians, renowned authors, scientists, teachers, nurses, artists, counselors, accountants, etc. I have had the great opportunity to witness many people transform on their mats. If I had to bet on it, I'd say that in some way, they brought their peaceful practices back to their families, students, patients, employees, bosses, customers and clients. I have observed and assisted others as they became yoga teachers, many processing their heartfelt life stories as I had started to do in my years of unfolding with Melanie and on my yoga mat. Individuals who process their dreams, worries, and fears are more likely to progress authentically with their emotions in the future.

Elevating the teacher within is how I started my first online "Conscious Connections Course" for soul-searching human beings, newbie yoga teachers, and health and wellness professionals. Proceeding with confidence by bringing their energy to community centers, places of worship, schools, businesses, and so on because the world needs more peacemakers, and this begins with us. I suspect that you too would welcome a spiritual, practical, kindhearted, powerful, intuitive being to teach your children, guide humanity, and be of service.

Each person is enhanced by those who cared for themselves while serving others. I have witnessed my behavior and been in the company of many incredible people who snap and get upset at the darndest things. Perhaps it's over who forgot to let the dog out last or why the toilet paper was put on "the wrong way," but truthfully, there's usually a more profound truth. If we yell because we're tired and learn from it, that's one thing. When we raise our voices and lose our temper repeatedly, even if it's occasionally in the privacy of our homes, we must question who we are and the meaning behind our outbursts. The more we tame ourselves, the better our world will be.

So much in life comes full circle. When traveling on Rock Road to my dearest Sheryl and Neil's studio – once nestled near a massive boulder believed to have been deposited by a glacier – I felt a pull that went beyond the physical destination. The experience of taking classes, training to become a teacher, and awakening my spirit lives on.

I was drawn closest to the essence of what makes me human through the extraordinary impressions, calibrations of movement, and shared lessons. Each intricate thread connected me to the worlds before and within me. The studio was more than a place; it was a bridging portal between the finite and infinite. It gave me tools not just to teach, but to live, question, and to connect with the eternal worlds I am yet to touch.

Online options arrived during the pandemic. A few months in I stepped away from teaching classes and workshops as I had in person for ten-plus years. Some of my routines went by the wayside; others stimulated my consciousness. In the expansion, boundless energy remained in addition to their eventual physical space relocation. In the collective rebound, a sizzle stirred when my beloved Naturally Yoga community announced a trip to Ireland. As an alternative to their previous journeys to India, this was presented as a magical, mystical European experience.

A few months later, I left lugging a black suitcase and carry-on, eager to journey alone with some I knew and others I had never met. In my first accommodation, I stayed in a drafty converted stable room. It was a renovated space and strange compared to some who stayed in the main house, but I felt the horse energy around me when I showered in what was once their water trough. Even stranger might be the energetic conversation I had with another uncle who had passed away earlier that year, a family doctor for fifty years and a horseman. I had come a long way since my hostel stay back in college! I was exploring once again with visionary eyes. We practiced yoga, went forest bathing, visited mysterious places like the Dingle Peninsula and ancient sites, ate farm-to-table food, and toured and stayed at family-owned estate gardens. Upon visiting one castle with a friend while others stayed closer to food and shopping, we walked through many unnerving archways and steps. Once we got to the top, I looked down and felt a bit weary, yet I went for the chance to kiss the Blarney Stone. After hearing many folklore tales about its good luck, it was finally checked off my bucket list. I was elated and tickled further when our group ate in a pub one evening, and I sipped a half-pint of Guinness for old time's sake.

A little backstory on Neil: he served in the Navy and ended up in New Jersey, where he met Sheryl by chance, and they married. One day, he picked up a book from Sheryl's nightstand. As part of her Integral Yoga Teacher Training, she was required to read Swami Satchidananda's commentary on *The Yoga Sutras of Patanjali* (Appendix). Absorbed in stories of the past offering guidance for the present, Neil became a skilled warrior in his own right. Overcoming inner battles and gaining insights into his past anger issues and upbringing from many sacred texts, another being the *Bhagavad Gita*.

Being a male presence in the mostly female yoga community, he served as a counterbalance and calming force. It's worth noting that yoga began with men, and now we are no longer cave-dwellers but inhabitants of a vibrant world. He doesn't bend like a pretzel on the yoga mat but is a true yogi and divine meditation teacher. As a jack-of-all-trades, in addition to his sacred text *Jnana* (wisdom knowledge), he includes *yoga nidra* (a sleep relaxation technique), laughing meditation, and mudras as direct cords from our hearts with others.

From his recent Facebook post:

> *"Staying positive doesn't mean you must always be happy. It means that even on the hardest days you know that better ones are coming."*

Sheryl, his better half (just kidding), reminded me yesterday after I rested my body to receive her Reiki energy healing to prioritize self love/care. We all need friends, mentors, and support systems to keep us from slipping off our routine tracks. To help others we must conquer and validate our quest to heal our hearts and souls.

Metamorphosis Informant

Stay aware, if you dare
of both the buzzing bee and the one you want others to see.
Let breath awareness serve as your guide,
Mitigate ardently, own your radiance like a rare butterfly.

Inhale to feel your heart's home,
Exhale to the sound of Om.

No(body) can take our peace away unless we give it to them!

You are of organic origin, an original formula life force, full of consciousness.

Purging trauma and drama with breath practices modifies each flurry of emotion as our mood swings. When the Radiant

Woman infuses awareness's powerful essence, she rises with the sun and calms as the moon dims daily.

Listen to birdsong, meditate on our breath by counting on the inhalation and exhalation to help us remain calm.

Use laughter and tears as medicine to blow off steam.

Mantra to Pollinate Transformation

I am not my body
I am not my mind
I am a radiant woman – powerful, calm, kind, and
compassionate,

A blissful spiritual being.
I embody the grace of light, love, freedom, and nature.

You are not your body
You are not your mind
You are a radiant woman – powerful, calm, kind, and
compassionate,

A blissful spiritual being.
You embody the grace of light, love, freedom, and nature.

We are not our bodies
We are not our minds
We are radiant women – powerful, calm, kind, and
compassionate,

Blissful spiritual beings.
We embody the grace of light, love, freedom, and nature.

Let this above mantra (or create one that speaks to your heart) spread like wildflowers. Write positive thoughts and intentions on "post-it" notes. Read mantra affirmations aloud. Place uplifting words and intentional phrases inside cupboards, on a bathroom mirror, fridge, or in your car. Turn the positivity formula into a way of life.

And just like the magic from new or older star formations that come together and open, the gravitational influence of giant molecular clouds can be disrupted over time as they move through the galaxy. Through space, even though some are gravitationally bound, stellar formations move.

We are star clusters, some more visible to the naked eye than others. Amazing people, brilliant when we stand alone, brighter when we shine together. From sunrise to sunset, moonbeams and beyond…

In this world of weather patterns, *Farmer's Almanac* predictions, and tidal waves, the only thing anyone can genuinely predict, orchestrate, and improve upon is their temperament and internal temperature.

Going numb (briefly) while parenting and experiencing the frustration of lack, even though it appeared I had it all, caused me to neglect my emotional state temporarily. When unforeseen health issues arose, I gracefully moved through the discomfort. My secret insecurity regarding my husband's devotion made me fall deeper in love with myself.

And just when I thought the luck of the Irish would end, Jonathan met me in Paris. I feel fortunate to have partnered with a man who loves to explore and apply astute expertise to everything he does (e.g., making travel arrangements, being meticulous with handiwork, a great concert and show ticket finder, an incredible researcher when it comes to helping our friends and family when purchasing cars or fixing something, and the list goes on). I wouldn't go to him for dentistry or soulful advice, and he's not asking me for a yoga sequence or a reiki healing, but I do stretch him when his muscles get tight. Intimacy crafts our caring partnership.

When we butt heads, he asks if I'm on the same team as him. Working with someone who wants to make all the decisions without being questioned can be challenging, but I acknowledge that he is usually precise and accurate. This doesn't mean we can't express our frustration or provide opinions. Ultimately, I appreciate his efforts. Our friction seems to rub the not-so-good stuff away so we can dote on each other.

November 10, 2009, a journal entry from my yoga teacher training said:

"Jonathan is out of touch with deep feelings but enjoys life to the fullest. As I embrace myself, I hope to influence my partner over the days, weeks, and years as we grow in love. He is very positive and takes in a lot with great pride."

We can never fully know another but can profess our love with raw, uncanniness. The pandemic wheels rotated extraneous grips on what we thought life would be. When we seize an opportune moment or gradually emerge from a cocooned state, we can acknowledge the big elephant in the room (our egos) and admire it with wonder, discovery, hope and joy for incidental aftermaths. Through this revamp, we gather momentum to appreciate and cherish the things that matter most.

Although I have sometimes lost my sense of identity, this has pushed me to broaden my perspective and return with determination.

Why had I, like many women I had known, felt powerless in the company of certain people's presence and yet brilliant and uplifted in other circles/communities?

My cherished grammar school friend Jacqueline Beth traveled across state borders to attend my first "official" bliss yoga demo class, which meant the world to me. Aside from the yoga community and a few of my kids, she was the only one who showed up. Supportive of my passion, plus gaining some calm for herself. Despite going for months without talking and even years without seeing each other, we nod when we speak and listen with no agenda. One day, we were at the Whitney Museum in Manhattan and had a heart-to-heart conversation while sitting on a bench. She listened as I divulged family riffs, causing tension between strong-minded relatives. It was easy to talk with someone who understood my long standing family dynamics. Not everyone is meant to hear our stories, yet finding a way to release them, write them, and be resourceful in calming our nervous systems so we can progress with intuitive radiance is beneficial for our health and wellness journeys.

I'm grateful for her unequivocal support. We have an unconditional support system rooted in our shared past and appreciation for each other's future. But isn't this the purpose of our lives? To connect with others, gain new perspectives from people we trust, and, most importantly, find outlets that help us - whether it's dancing at a party, tossing a ball with a friend or child, playing casually or on a professional stage, court, or field. Hand-eye coordination and playing games like Back-gammon (my parent's favorite from when we were young), Boggle, and Wordle, sharpen our minds and keep us in the moment. Hence, we know when to step out of the way before an emotional landslide crashes.

Why had it appeared to everyone else's eyes that I was just fine when something inside of me broke down and felt off balance?

When considering your sense of self, a common question is, "Who am I?"

I could slow down and quiet my thoughts by practic-ing postures and contemplation amid the noise. Each time I entered and left *Naturally Yoga*, I felt more at ease. This disciplined practice, over time, brought me to uncover my pure essence. By intertwining the *yamas* (values to live by), I rededicated my life with a higher determination to become self-actualized.

We can live an exceptional quality of life by shedding the complex roles of womanhood and finding peace, serenity, and bliss on the other side of chaos.

Even idle gossip can damage someone's reputation or career or make a permanent or hard-to-remove mark. Once words project from our mouths, we can never take them back.

Little white lies and misaligned inside voices reveal conse-quences, harming the speaker as much as its target, even if she didn't intend to diminish someone else's shine.

The Radiant Woman finds grace and joy through life's ups and downs. When mental and physical health challenges arise, she searches for alternative solutions, unearthing and exploring botanicals and herbs, magic potions and charms, and traditional and nontraditional medicinal practices to lore. Her facial expression and actions portray happiness and fulfillment, oriented toward actualizing her life's purpose.

When we focus on love, more love blossoms.

Let's take a moment to soothe our minds before sending messages to others. Aim to communicate with heartfelt intentions. Reflect on our words and refrain from responding with rebuttals that could tarnish our relationships. Communicate with soulful, sincere respect and kindness using words that bring us together rather than apart. It's like two lovebirds taking flight to prosper and soar. Apologize for our part in the argument, as any higher source of Godly power, including yourself, will hear your plea.

As we welcome change, shifts happen (and might turn out better than expected).

With each sunset we rest, each sunrise is an opportunity to rewrite and redirect our stories to create a new environment that breeds pure goodness. It's not if, but when, the light goes dim, she trusts that her radiance will perk up and be restored, blossoming like a sunflower – hardy and long-stemmed.

In 2015, I participated in an "Art and Yoga" intensive at Kripalu with Joan Hanley. It was the last time she would teach this well-known and sought-after program as it had been for years at that location. I had heard about it and didn't want to miss the opportunity to learn from her, so I packed my yoga pants and headed again to Lenox. I woke before 5 a.m. for a cold shower and the optional *sadhana*. We meditated as the sun rose, ate breakfast in silence, danced, practiced yoga *kriyas*, mingled, and painted throughout the days when prompted. Our five-foot paper canvases were adhered on the walls with blue painter's tape. During breaks, I often stayed back to add more color and adjust my abstract painting, even after others had left for meals or free time. I had no idea what I was doing. Energy ran through me. It was a great experience and helped me explore my artistic side. As the days went on when people gazed at my painting, some asked where I went to art school, yet it was the first time I had ever painted as an adult, except for my kid's paint-and-play and once when I fiddled with my sister's art supplies the year I graduated college.

During quarantine, I rediscovered an old canvas in my basement and decided to use Ben's long-forgotten acrylic paints and table easel. I also noticed strawberries in a green quart and sunflowers in a vase in my kitchen, so I tried painting them. I honed in, added details and mixed colors, and redid the 3-D conceptual depth and loose lines multiple times.

A few months after my first attempt, I tried painting again. I made bigger brushstrokes this time and created a big heart with abstract lines. When my mother-in-law asked where I planned to hang the sunflower piece, I felt both paintings looked average, so I set them aside for about a year.

While returning with my family from our annual trip to Ogunquit, Maine, I texted astrologer Wendy because I felt unsettled at the end of the trip.

We scheduled a perfectly timed meeting, as my birthday was approaching soon. She asked if I had any creative passions I'd like to pursue. Your charts reveal exploration of some sort in the arts before you proceed in how you're meant to support prospective clients through your yoga lifestyle business.

I told her about my one-time painting in Massachusetts and the two canvases I fiddled with during the pandemic. I expressed my desire to try oil and paint on a large canvas like at Kripalu.

"With your birthday approaching," she urged, "purchase a canvas; to create is NOW!"

Hubby hung a seven-by-four canvas in my garage. Without knowing what to do next, I started painting with delighted passion, vented many frustrations, and burned negative energy away with my garage door open. Birds chirping and a new rhythm exploded in me. "Where's Mom?" the kids asked when home. I was staying up late at night and rising early to add a detail. While completing it, I intermittently started dancing to a nearby three-by-five blank canvas already hung on the wall and painted over certain parts of those two original smaller canvases. I wanted to bring resurgence to them. When Hubby's Aunt Jan visited, she said the large one looked like "surrealism." I called it "The Universe." It seemed a miraculous piece had emerged. Vanessa was with me in every brushstroke. Emotions bubbling inside of me…

A few months later, I dedicated a painting to Mom for a healing shift after her single mastectomy removal of lymph nodes from breast cancer. As I neared its completion, I added a lotus flower rising from a leaf pad on a two-inch stem (I was patient with myself in the refinement until I felt the water and tonalities were just right). Jonathan surprised my parents with its installation. When the war in Ukraine erupted, I painted a mountainous scene imbued with eyes of humane sensitivities. The volatile situation kept me agile on the canvas. I have more to express, share, create, write, and paint, and I will continue to favor ways to release stress to purify my mind. And that is my message for you too.

How can we let go of our troubles and allow them to pass through us until they disappear?

We evolve with increased capableness when we believe in ourselves, develop a versatile range of skills and talents, and stay aware of our surroundings.

For all my worries, witnessing my children climb ever higher mountains - sometimes stumbling when the terrain gets rough but always standing up after the fall - brings me tears of gratification. All beings, to one degree or another, are left to fend for themselves, and it is always up to the individual to rebuild life as they go from childhood to adulthood. Even if one or both parents/guardians set up the original foundations, it is our life's work to undo, grow, and evolve. Moving from lament to light in any relationship generates both pleasure and pain. When we improve our mental capacity, reconstruct our physical state, surrender to the temporary impermanence of our lives, and learn how to orchestrate the mystery of our inner and outer environments, we learn to relish our victories. We notice what's possible on the other side of any challenge.

My temple's previous rabbi used to arrange small round-table discussions on social action and mitzvah (doing good deeds, conscious acts of empathy) projects. She emphasized that one's career path, job title, or educational degree - whether as a student, landscaper, journalist, banker, doctor, lawyer, maintenance/contract worker, baker, teacher, therapist, beekeeper, inventor and so on - is not remembered as one's standout feature. According to her, what truly matters is an individual's character strength. Do you treat yourself with kindness and compassion? What can you do today to cultivate joy despite calamities? How can you be authentic while making others feel comfortable?

What does depression mean? My husband's grandmother, Nana Ruth, was a strong and radiant woman who believed that only those who lived through the Great Depression could truly understand the meaning of life. And while she asked me about the prices of essentials like eggs and milk, I was grateful that I didn't have to worry about affording them, yet I listened intently to her words. Although our experiences were different, we shared the common trait of being women who understood that suffering is necessary to appreciate happiness. Papa Harold was meticulous when eating a row of corn and shucking it.

One of his memorable responses when we presented him with our endless list of household repairs was, "Poor people don't have those problems." That sure did put things in perspective. We were and are fortunate to wake up in a warm bed, have our cupboards and fridge filled with fresh produce and ingredients, and be able to pay if something warrants fixing. Sure, our experiences were different, but this allowed us to ease our frustration when we faced temporary householder challenges. But from this, a bigger question arose.

What does it truly mean to be poor? Can feeling hopeless and over-whelmed by life's obstacles lead to deplorable states? If so, are we brave enough to overcome what seems impossible? Can we inhabit the radical Zen we left behind?

Taking responsibility for our sometimes myopic and ignorant opinions allows us to develop personal relationships founded on respecting others' boundaries. If we have a light side over-shadowed by our wounded child, we can still explore how it felt being controlled or not paid attention to at one time or another by a parental or authoritative figure. Ascend like a butterfly, morphing through cosmic connections. Aspiring to higher accolades, achieving more incredible accomplishments. Adopting new behaviors to restructure familiar habits that no longer serve us. Living a notch out of traditional "accepted" politically and medically plotted systems. Inscribing our epitaph while alive, crafting the timeless act of legacy for future generations offering hope, trust, and respect with shared meaning for centuries to come.

The Art of Radiance

Like most people, at first, I figured I'd go to yoga to stretch, relax and come back a little more toned; everything changed once I stoked a conscious connection turning point. Not only was I capturing spurts of newfound joy before, during, and after a yoga class, but my entire internal landscape shifted so much that I felt like I was floating on Cloud 9, living the high life in ways I never imagined. By shedding layers of my past, I was able to leave behind erroneous "crap" stories I created in my mind and become the Radiant Woman I was meant to be.

The Radiant Woman: When opposition arises, she accepts the challenge, taps into her resourcefulness to access equilibrium, and dissolves dueling polarities in her relationships – a never-ending cycle. This brilliant woman notices perfection in the uneven sidewalk cracks as a metaphor for the splintered beauty of each moment, giving reason to her individuality and natural radiant glow.

Process: She reframes her mind through The Radiant Woman's Way, retrains her body to envelop exaltation and peaceful energy experiences, and returns to inspired states of being.

She inserts "The 5M's of Meditation" into her life to brighten her days:

1. Movement shifts
2. Music for the soul
3. Mantra affirmations
4. Mudra gestures
5. Magical integration

The Radiant Woman turns hardships into teachable opportunities for future wisdom, purifying her thoughts and remaining calm by reducing tension barriers. She accesses all temperamental elements within herself through nature's lifeforce energy and moves through temporary emotional commotion.

Discomfort: When we experience something uncomfortable, we can invoke Energy Awareness Tools (EAT – nourishing your heart's content) to dismantle old belief systems and wake up with radiance.

LETTER TO MY READERS

Dear Radiant Woman,

What image do you see when you gaze at your reflection? How are you perceived by others when they see you?

You are amazing!
I am amazing!
We are amazing!

Even if you don't feel amazing in the moment, you can retrain your brain.

Why not treat today as an opportunity to explore, congregate, contemplate, and shine?

Take a trip to your local coffee shop, art exhibit, musical concert, or park bench. Observe the people around you to notice the marvel in all beings.

Meditate in tidbit increments throughout your day by following the breath through your nostrils. Elongate inhalation and exhalation, bringing airflow to your diaphragm's lower regions.

This simple yet powerful act has been scientifically proven to create new neuropathways. It allows you to live without attachment to one emotional state because this moment of joy or pain will pass in time.

It's time to give yourself some grace.

Learn or discover uncovered passions brewing inside. Tailor the frequency of your thoughts to feel your best self, even during tough times.

Restraining from gossip is an excellent way to build and develop positive character traits. A gentler voice of reason is recognized as truth. Like trees and flowers blooming without expectation of being noticed, the evolution of relationships is influenced by cyclical exchange.

Reflecting on yesterday's mishaps to improve your relations for a better tomorrow is a circle back in the right direction. It comes around to remind you of what has not yet been resolved. It takes time to mend, wake up, and do this thing called life, again and again.

You matter, as does the person with an opposing position or force. If your words will not lift someone (including yourself), refrain and reframe. Pause before speaking. When you turn your power charge cord on to filter out what doesn't serve you and lean into what motivates you, you add value to your relationship with yourself and others.

Bake, sing, paint, play, dance, sew, swim, knit, craft, design, hike, bike, walk, write, run, laugh.

Consider volunteering your time for meaningful causes and remember to check in with a friend who may be struggling. A simple phone call could make all the difference. Helping another can beat many depressive states away, for you as well as them.

Be compassionate towards past versions of yourself, whether from last week, last year, or many moons ago. Notice the magnificent, super-powerful, brilliant woman you've grown into today.

Be patient as you await the apple to naturally ripen from the tree (a concept I learned from my yoga studies). Luxuriate in the sweet nectar of life by savoring simple, subtle moments.

Magnify your radiance in this lifetime so you don't go to sleep on your last day with regret for what you missed out on. Instead, bring goodness to others by first caring for your inner world.

In the land of make-believe, we can aim our love arrow where we want it to go; the remolded energy informs the electrical current of misbeliefs to be overshadowed by newer, more valuable beliefs.

Be the freedom warrior to live the life that inspires your visions.

Curiosity and spiritual awakenings are callings led by choice. The human experience was never meant to be easy. Once you taste spiritual sweetness, hidden gems rooted in happiness exceed your expectations.

It's okay to experience turmoil and rise again in sisterhood. Call on your feminine light. Harness your masculine side too.

Do whatever it takes to access your rockstar caliber, fairy dust peace. Let it linger and shine for eternity.

The gift of love is your presence!

You have gained a friend in me. I hope my stories, gentle yogi whispers, and reflections on clutter and decay remind you that you too can recover.

Be grateful for each fleeting moment. Look ahead and appreciate your body for the graceful temple that it is. Sprinkle colorful vitality and calm into your days as a formula to age gracefully.

May each adventure, contemplative chapter, and prompt in this book be a resource for you to dialogue with amongst friends and family. If you feel called to, revisit any stories, opening up to any chapter for the courage to persist or resist.

Open your angelic wingspans wider than ever imagined before. Take flight with courageousness.

As incredible as it is or might be to travel and visit natural wonders and historical sites, you never have to go too far if you want to find joy. Doing whatever it takes to feel at peace is your ultimate birthright.

Yes, you have imagined or gone underwater to investigate dark oceans and flown high like a soaring bird in the sky. Not only do your mysterious ventures mimic the vast blue skies, wondrous sun, cloud, moon, forests, air, fire, and water elements outside, all of life's existence can be found within. There's infinite space for soul-to-soul connections as they relate to influencing human conditions and behavior to support and uplift one another.

Love, kindness, and treating others how you want to be treated is your lifeline. Taking care of yourself as you care for others is The Radiant Woman's Way.

When you paint your dream scenes like masterful artists and dedicate your days to prioritizing what matters most, you receive a massive blessing. When we feel a solid connection to our existence, we can make subtle but meaningful impacts on the Universe.

Make space for wild wonders to present themselves through gentle whispers to stillness, for exalted states of bliss to coexist in the tumult of life, for it's in the clearing gunk where your superconscious connection roars.

When faced with a problem, ask yourself what the situation is trying to teach you. Try to look at those painful blisters through a spiritual lens. Develop your inner wisdom and seek guidance from professionals such as mental health experts, mentors, clergy members, spiritual guides, and healing practitioners who can offer alternative ways to express yourself. Allowing yourself to detach from disturbances can help your conscience listen to your heart's intuition.

You are whole, wholesome, and pure as you are.

Seasonal Moods Change

> *Winter blues, chilling reels.*
> *Spring action, tulip fields,*
> *Summer's heat, swelter sweats*
> *Falling leaves, autumn begets.*

A windy breeze swiftly bends,
Lively seasons repeat again
Mood fluctuations- atone, prepare,
Becoming attuned and self-aware.

Sticky sneezes, hay fever miffed.
Just like the dampened weather, emotional feathers drift.
Erroneous storms emoting tears.
Dredging; The Radiant Woman pioneers.

With lots of love and light from my heart's home space to yours,

You've got this, my friend!

It's your time to shine!

Big hugs!

Marla

The actionable, thought-provoking steps throughout the book are yours to revisit anytime as a formula to carve new pathways, create movement and change. You can go back to prior chapters' journal prompts and incorporate meditative moments and motivation into your days to indulge in the joys of life and be better primed for when presented with challenges

GLOSSARY

Sanskrit

Ananda: bliss

Bodhisattva: self-assured contentment

Bhakti: devotional love

Dharma: wisdom path of living, sustains order

Hatha yoga: slower-paced movements and stretching with a focus on breathing,

Kundalini: yoga of awareness

Karma: action deeds

Namaste: "The light in you mirrors the light in me."

Pranayama: life-force energy breathing practices

Patanjali Sutras: wisdom guidelines for living a meaningful and purposeful life

Svadhyaya: self-study

Santosha: contented truth

Upanishads: the unifying principle among apparent diversity in the cosmos

Vinyasa yoga: focuses on connecting breath to faster-paced, flowing movements.

Yoga: to join in union. Hindi mysticism *with exertion of body and mind*

Hebrew/Yiddish

Adon Alam: a hymn in the Jewish liturgy of awestruck reference for the "Eternal Lord"

Antisemitism: see Marla's Defamation Blog – marlasacks.com/part1-antisemitism

Kabbalah: Jewish tradition of mystical interpretation of the Bible

Kugel: Jewish sweet noodle pudding

L'dor'va dor: sharing sacredness from one generation to the next

Mitzvah: good deed or action

Mazel Tov: congratulations on a Simcha, lifecycle

Schmutz: messy

Shabbat: marks the Sabbath, a day for prayer blessing, community and rest

Shalom: a greeting for peace

Tikva: hope

ABOUT THE AUTHOR

Marla Sacks, a yoga and meditation mentor, was born in Philadelphia, Pennsylvania and raised in New Jersey, where she still resides. She is an artist, writer, and poet; a wife and mother of four; a daughter, sister, spiritual seeker, speaker, and a friend to many.

As an overwhelmed mom, Marla lost her way, which manifested emotionally and physically exacerbating autoimmune disorders. The Radiant Woman transformation began once mind-body-spirit influence emboldened her purpose. When one woman poses the grateful grace, she instills love and kindness to spark joy.

Marla weaves mini-moment pause practices and ancient yogic wisdom into her growth formulas, encouraging all beings to let go of yesterday's woes and reclaim their powerful presence. Her signature Radiance Resets offerings include: The Radiant Woman's Way Programs & Retreats; *The 5 M's to Meditation Micro-course: Mantra, Movement, Mudras* (hand gestures) *Meditations, and Magic; Conscious Connections Course* (designed for spiritual seekers: yoga/health and wellness enthusiasts/professionals, teachers/students, and therapists); and *Yoga Meditations and Social Skills Course for Tweens* in collaboration with Licensed Clinical Social Worker and Yoga Therapist, Amanda Sacks.

She enjoys entrepreneurial creation mode, spending time outdoors, experiencing natural landscapes, vegetation, and flowers, wandering in local parks, traveling to old and modern cities, and exploring sites with surprising historical richness and tantalizing cuisines.

She expresses herself through various activities, such as trying out new gourmet recipes, gardening, painting, reading historical fiction and self-help guides, indulging in spa-like wellness programs and fitness routines, spending time at the beach, hiking mountains, and being a student with other seekers of life. To sweeten the pot, spending quality time with her children, husband, friends and family, and cuddling with her golden Yorkie Mini makes her heart sing,

The Radiant Woman Shines is her first book.

ACKNOWLEDGMENTS

In gratitude to Sheryl and Neil Edsall of Naturally Yoga for opening their hearts and creating a conscious community that gives all beings an omnipresent space to breathe. Your individual and collective guidance in self-study, anatomy, and deep, connective spiritual love opened my imagination and reignited The Radiant Woman in me to progress.

To Jonathan, our amusement ride romance continues to lead me to greener pastures. I appreciate your partnership. It has enriched various aspects of my life, such as parenting, planting gardens to sow seeds, preparing my canvases before I paint, and framing them afterward. Becoming my astounding uber-assistant was paramount to helping me finish my book.

As for my four fabulous children, your obstacles, milestones, and pursuits have inspired me to grow wiser. Your unique hand and footprints are interlaced with my heartbeats. Amanda has shown a remarkable aptitude for spreading kindness. She became a yoga teacher at age sixteen and, later, a therapist. Her "We All Feel" platform reminds us to feel by illuminating what's real. Jeremy's knowledge of finance led him to save, invest, and become entrepreneurial. He is an effective communicator and sound advisor, using his words wisely for relationship-building. Benjamin studied law, which was reminiscent of his earliest days when he asked adults and peers relevant questions. He is resolute, unassuming, and ready to utilize his expertise to enhance policies and procedures. To our self-assured baby, Rachel, observing your athletic resilience as a competitive cheerleader, and your decision to pursue acupuncture after obtaining an undergraduate degree in molecular biology reminds me to follow what makes my heart sing.

I am grateful to my parents for allowing me to experience life's simple, peculiar, mysterious wonders. Dad, thanks for humoring me, reminding me never to eat yellow snow, and to let go of worry since everything will be okay ninety-nine percent of the time. Mom, your gentle presence reminds me to forgo any resentment for your advice. Thank you for being patient with me during my reactive teenage and young adult years. It has led me to magnificent glaciers, precious gemstones, fierce thunderstorms and, most of all, love.

To the clergy, my rabbis, and spiritual teachers who have the fortitude to inspire others with hope and love through their prolific teachings, I am blessed. Each has become a spiritual pillar for me to be me.

Next, I highlight my friends and family from different walks of life. So many of you have encouraged me to step out of my comfort zone to write this book and share some of my artistic, creative muses and visions with the world.

Ilene Sands, you are an incredible communicator, a lover of the arts, a cheerleader for all, a true radiant woman, my confidant, and a trusted friend. You have consistently supported my passion projects, and I am deeply grateful.

Heather Won Choi, your unwavering support inspires, uplifts, and empowers me to persevere and share my message as a reminder to all women to keep going. A radiant woman shines through the darkest nights of her soul and finds a way to spread joy, love, and respect for all.

For my art and yoga teacher, Joan Hanley, I feel your presence perched on my shoulder in my makeshift garage art studio. Thanks also to Ajeet and Mahan Kirn for making the world a more conscious place. Each was part of an invisible revival initiative to strengthen my pituitary gland and unleash my creativity. Thank you for your magnetic majesty.

With appreciation to Gail Sobel for her unwavering commitment to OB-GYN and women's health, a compassionate doctor. You're a true inspiration – an incredible mother and wife with a brilliant ability to follow your heart by integrating energy medicine and alternative healing modalities into your life. I wish you all the best in the next phase of radiance.

To my writing coach, Dawn Montefusco, who taught me the three Cs – Courage, Consistency and Compassion – as a formula for letting go of my inner critic. Naming it, thanking it for showing up, and then bidding it bye-bye has helped me confidently "get thoughts out of my head and onto the page." For my publishing team that influenced the crux of my storytelling – Dana Micheli, thank you for the sidenote recommendations for each round of manuscript editing. Shanda Trofe, I appreciate your brilliant, gentle nudges to make finishing this project a top priority and a reality.

CONTINUE THE JOURNEY

*If you would like to connect with Marla for a speaking
engagement or to bring the Radiant Woman program
and mini-retreat experience to a location near you visit:*

marlasacks.com

Radiance Bonus Gifts for My Readers

Congratulations on finishing *The Radiant Woman Shines!*

As a thank you, I've created exclusive Radiance Bonus Meditation demos for you to follow along with as a complement to your journey.

Click below to access:

- Video downloads
- Guided meditations
- Practices you can use anytime

These tools are designed to support your radiance and help you shine even brighter!

> ### Bonus Gifts:
> marlasacks.com/book-bonus-gift

Current offerings

To learn more about Marla and The 5 M's to Meditation Micro-Course, find her on Instagram, Facebook, YouTube, LinkedIn, and marlasacks.com/offerings.

Bring The Radiant Woman Program, mind, body, intuition wellness connection to a location near you.

APPENDIX

Creative Inceptions - Spiritual Wealth + Health:

Astrologer: Wendy Cicchetti: twixtearthandsky.com

Astrology - Danielle Mercurio: daniellemercurio.com

Ayurveda master/ gut health/ plant medicine/yogi: Sheryl Edsall: naturallyyoga.com

Ayurvedic spices: Chef Rama and Anita: satyablends.com

Back on Track Lifestyle and Exercise Guide on Healing Back Pain by Roberta Bergman: amzn.to/3RA0a1I

Big Magic: Creative Living Beyond Fear by Elizabeth Gilbert: amzn.to/4crbW6y

Buried Treasures by Guru Singh: hamzn.to/3VOU2Ff

Cracking the Resistance Code: How to Break Through Fear of Uncertainty and Write Your Book by Dawn Montefusco: amzn.to/3VOUpQ9

Ho'oponopono: The Hawaiian Ritual of Forgiveness by Ulrich F. Duprée: amzn.to/4ldrUVO

In the Lotus of the Heart by Shubhraji: inthelotusoftheheart.com

Remember Love by Cleo Wade:

amazon.com/Remember-Love-Words-Tender-Times/dp/0593581369

Sweat: Uncovering Your Body's Hidden Superpower by Justin Glaser: amzn.to/3VPcEVB

The Bhagavad Gita: A Walkthrough for Westerners by Jack Hawley a.co/d/cQajmUu

The Secret Power of Yoga: A Woman's Guide to the Heart and Spirit of the Yoga Sutras by Nischala Joy Devi: amzn.to/4cuTeeo

The War of Art: Break Through the Blocks and Win Your Inner Creative Battles by Steven Pressfield: a.co/d/aKC6PYw

The Yoga Sutras of Patanjali, commentary by Swami Satchidananda: a.co/d/cu6Hnld

Wabi Sabi Love by Arielle Ford: amzn.to/45A5acD

Jin Shin Jutzu®: suzanneabarron.com

Life - Writing - Business - Coaching

Dawn Montefusco: dawnmontefusco.com

Kathe Crawford: kathecrawford.com

Sarah Walton: sarahwalton.com

Publishing Guidance + Services: shandatrofe.com

Integrative Modalities

Annalisa Pastore (Chi Medicine): chi-medicine.com/staff

The Biology of Beliefs by Dr. Bruce Lipton: amazon. com/Biology-Belief-10th-Anniversary-Consciousness/dp/140195247X

Kula for Karma: kulaforkarma.org

Meditation - Yoga - Spiritual Guides (virtual and in-person)

Intuitive Healer + Reiki Guide - Lorin Oneal: instagram. com/lifehealingwithlorinoneal

Intuition Guide - Christine Brown: claritywithchristine.com

Gurmukh: goldenbridgeyoga.com

Ho-Ho-Kus Yoga: hohokusyoga.com

Moon Magic Reiki: moonmagicwellness.com/about

Yoga + Meditation Center - Neil Edsall and Sheryl Edsall: naturallyyoga.com

Shubhraji: namahom.org

Healer + Blue Lotus Healing School - Mahani: mahankirn.com

Tapping Method for Anxiety: thetappingsolution.com

Tova Yoga - Rachel Dewan: yogatova.com/jewish-yoga

Yoga Synthesis: yogasynthesis.com

Lifestyle Retreats

Kripalu: kripalu.org

Omega: eomega.org

Foundation

Pediatric Brain Tumors Research: ironmatt.org

Mental Health Resources

Addiction

From Chaos to Clarity, Seeing the Signs and Breaking the Cycles by Marci Hopkins: amzn.to/3VtV6x7

Marci Hopkins: wakeupwithmarci.com

Grief

Reiki Master - Eileen Alexander: eileenalexander.com

Psychotherapy - Support Groups

Amanda Sacks Therapy - We All Feel: amandasacks.com

Melanie Struble: bodypositiveworks.com/therapy-counseling-bergen-county-nj/

Suicide Prevention & Walks: afsp.org
Life After Suicide by Dr. Jennifer Ashton: amzn.to/3RvYN3V

Music

a. Ajeet: ajeetmusic.com

b. Meditation and Chakra Healing Music: youtu.be/ZQkBmCJ G9i8?si=kiZ-GAVhtiHAI75S

c. Kirtan Kriya Sa Ta Na Ma Music:
   - youtube.com/watch?v=QDL_ZV5acTs
   - youtu.be/Zg9NOOM2neA?si=ti2H0Lx_apc2L1RN

d: Penni Feiner music https://music.apple.com/us/artist/penni-feiner/956464692

The Arts - Travel - Nutrition - Style

Acupuncture + Wellbeing - Rachel Sacks: instagram.com/wellnesswithray_

Art Enthusiast /Representative - Ilene Sands: instagram.com/artbyilene

Art and Yoga - Hari Kirn: a.co/d/fq9yHnc

Art Shows + Mentorship - Joan Haney: hanleystudio.com

Fave Chocolate: mishti-chocolates.com

Jewels - Custom Designed: etsy.com/shop/FacetsEtcBy-Nancy; Instagram.com/facets.etc

Jewelry - Love In a Bracelet: loveinabracelet.com

Fitness and Nutrition - Kristin Reed: charisfitnessnj.com

Hair and Meditation: hairdo-lini.com

Honest Fashion and Accessories for Moms/Women: Katie Sands: instagram.com/itskatiesands

Nutrition Programs for Women - Audrey Zona: LiveZoHealthy.com

Organizer - Lori Bailey: missorganizednj.com

Organized systems/books - Shira Gill: shiragill.com

Photographer - Jen Bladel: villagestudiophotos.com

Stylist - Soneca Guadara: stylebysoneca.com

RADIANT REFLECTIONS BOOK CLUB DISCUSSION QUESTIONS

After reading *The Radiant Woman Shines*, I hope you found time to engage in the prompts after each chapter. The radiant reflection questions allow you to delve deeper into discussions for personal introspection, book clubs, and women's groups. To keep the conversations going, Marla is available to join book clubs and speak on topics related to The Radiant Woman's Way. Plus, there's more on her website and blog at **MarlaSacks. com**.

- During a pivotal moment in Marla's motherhood bustle, she loses her grip and cries at the steering wheel. Reflect on a time when your life seemed too overwhelming.

- Marla called her first method of dealing with emotional overwhelm the cover-up period. Have you ever gone through the motions of life in a state of numbness where you hid your emotional pain?

- After feeling misunderstood by her husband Jon and later embarrassed for seeing a therapist, Marla begins to uncover her buried emotions. Have you ever felt uneasy about expressing your emotions alone, with a partner, therapist, or in public?

- Marla used to make herself available to any friend, family member, or coworker who asked for her attention before tending to herself. Has the busyness of caretaking or nurturing careers, including motherhood, ever led you to forget to care for yourself?

- Marla's journey highlights how detoxing from internal and external conversations, alongside spiritual practices like yoga, Reiki, and conscious community, can become essential for self-care and growth. What non-negotiable rituals or practices help you stay grounded and aligned in your daily life?

- Since the pandemic, tending to our mental health emotions when it comes to crises such as grief, overcoming addiction and suicide prevention has become even more acceptable. Even with social media and emotional disruptions, are we as a human species evolving in consciousness by helping another (including ourselves), and can we flow in alignment to access more joy in our lives, despite the noise?

- In *The Radiant Woman Shines*, Marla becomes a friend to herself while embracing and strengthening her powerful essence. As her perspective on letting go of what's beyond her control, along with discipline and forgiveness, shifted, she took ownership of her emotions and learned to accept her husband and others, despite their differences. Discuss how becoming a friend to yourself, rather than blaming others, can serve as a valuable tool for enhancing relationships.

- In her first job, Marla worked as an art consultant with aspirations of opening her own gallery. Though she later set aside her creative projects, she eventually rediscovered her path in new and fulfilling ways. Have you ever set aside a dream or intuitive insight, only to return to it – or discover something even more aligned – later in life? How did it reshape your sense of purpose or creativity?

- In the East Meets West chapter, Marla shares her struggles with autoimmune conditions and long-term Lyme disease, delving into the integration of conventional medicine with natural remedies. How do you see this holistic approach influencing your family's journey to better health and contributing to a broader, more universal approach to wellness?

- Marla values the friendships she has made throughout her life, recognizing the importance of women supporting one another, refraining from gossip, and fostering self-compassion as a formula to shine. How have the friends in your life – both old and new – influenced your radiance, and what can you do today to cultivate being a "good, loving" friend to your higher conscious self?

- Marla shares her experiences with a spontaneous tandem flight, exploring the ocean's depths, climbing, biking, speaking up for her beliefs, and more. When have you shown courage in your own life – whether in a relationship, a sport, or standing up for something you believed in or advocated for?

- Antisemitism via Marla's father's case and the poker chip story is a thread that inspires her to persevere and step outside of her box for being different. Has being bullied or cast out encouraged or defeated a dream of yours?

- Does becoming a mood barometer, as Marla demonstrates in her personal development through the ebb and flow of life, resonate with you? Can you relate to the idea of "when it rains, it pours," and the importance of accessing tools to navigate emotional storms and cultivate inner peace?

- Marla prioritizes finding peace and accessing joy. Reflect on how adopting a bird's-eye view or watching life as though it were a movie – where you are a spectator with a broadened perspective – can elevate humanity. How might this shift invite you to lighten up and access your true radiance?

www.ingramcontent.com/pod-product-compliance
Lightning Source LLC
Chambersburg PA
CBHW061604120626
46550CB00004B/1615